PRACTICE - ASSESS - DIAG

180 Days of READING for Kindergarten

Author
Suzanne Barchers, Ed.D.

SHELL EDUCATION

Contributing Author

Jodene Smith, M.A.

Publishing Credits

Dona Herweck Rice, *Editor-in-Chief*; Robin Erickson, *Production Director*;
Lee Aucoin, *Creative Director*; Timothy J. Bradley, *Illustration Manager*;
Conni Medina, M.A.Ed., *Editorial Director*; Sara Johnson, M.S.Ed., *Senior Editor*;
Aubrie Nielsen, M.S.Ed., *Editor*; Grace Alba, *Designer*; Alison Berry, *Illustrator*;
Maple Lam, *Illustrator*; Stephanie Reid, *Photo Editor*;
Corinne Burton, M.A.Ed., *Publisher*

Image Credits

Cover, Maple Lam; p. 120 istock; p. 216 National Geographic Images/Copyright © Cyril Ruoso/ JH Editorial / Minden Pictures;
all other images Shutterstock

Standards

© 2004 Mid-continent Research for Education and Learning (McREL)
© 2007 Teachers of English to Speakers of Other Languages, Inc. (TESOL)
© 2007 Board of Regents of the University of Wisconsin System. World-Class Instructional Design and Assessment
    (WIDA). For more information on using the WIDA ELP Standards, please visit the WIDA website at www.wida.us.
© 2010 National Governors Association Center for Best Practices and Council of Chief State School Officers (CCSS)

Shell Education

5301 Oceanus Drive
Huntington Beach, CA 92649-1030
http://www.shelleducation.com

ISBN 978-1-4258-0921-8

©2013 Shell Education Publishing, Inc.

The classroom teacher may reproduce copies of materials in this book for classroom use only. The reproduction of any part
for an entire school or school system is strictly prohibited. No part of this publication may be transmitted, stored, or recorded
in any form without written permission from the publisher.

TABLE OF CONTENTS

INTRODUCTION AND RESEARCH

The Need for Practice

In order to be successful in today's reading classroom, students must deeply understand both concepts and procedures so that they can discuss and demonstrate their understanding. Demonstrating understanding is a process that must be continually practiced in order for students to be successful. According to Marzano, "practice has always been, and always will be, a necessary ingredient to learning procedural knowledge at a level at which students execute it independently" (2010, 83). Practice is especially important to help students apply reading comprehension strategies and word-study skills.

Understanding Assessment

In addition to providing opportunities for frequent practice, teachers must be able to assess students' foundational reading skills. This is important so that teachers can adequately address students' misconceptions, build on their current understanding, and challenge them appropriately. Assessment is a long-term process that often involves careful analysis of student responses from a lesson discussion, a project, a practice sheet, or a test. When analyzing the data, it is important for teachers to reflect on how their teaching practices may have influenced students' responses and to identify those areas where additional instruction may be required. In short, the data gathered from assessments should be used to inform instruction: slow down, speed up, or reteach. This type of assessment is called *formative assessment*.

HOW TO USE THIS BOOK

180 Days of Reading for Kindergarten offers teachers and parents a full page of daily foundational reading practice activities for each day of the school year.

Easy to Use and Standards Based

These activities reinforce grade-level skills across a variety of reading concepts. The questions are provided as a full practice page, making them easy to prepare and implement as part of a classroom morning routine, at the beginning of each reading lesson, or as homework. The weekly focus alternates between fiction and nonfiction standards.

Every kindergarten practice page provides questions that are tied to a reading or writing standard. Students are given the opportunity for regular practice in foundational reading skills, allowing them to build confidence through these quick standards-based activities.

Question	Common Core State Standards
Days 1–3	
1–3	**Reading Foundational Skills 3a:** *Demonstrate basic knowledge of letter-sound correspondences by producing the primary or most frequent sound for each consonant* **or** **Reading Foundational Skills 3b:** *Associate the long and short sounds with the common spellings (graphemes) for the five major vowels.*
4	**Reading Foundational Skills 3d:** *Distinguish between similarly spelled words by identifying the sounds of the letters that differ.*
Day 4	
1–4	**Reading Foundational Skills 4:** *Read emergent-reader texts with purpose and understanding.*
Day 5	
	Writing 3: *Use a combination of drawing, dictating, and writing to narrate a single event or several loosely linked events, tell about the events in the order in which they occurred, and provide a reaction to what happened.*

         © Shell Education

HOW TO USE THIS BOOK *(cont.)*

Using the Practice Pages

Practice pages provide instruction and assessment opportunities for each day of the school year. The activities are organized into weekly themes, and teachers may wish to prepare packets of each week's practice pages for students. Days 1, 2, and 3 follow a consistent format, with matching activities. As outlined on page 4, every item is aligned to a reading standard.

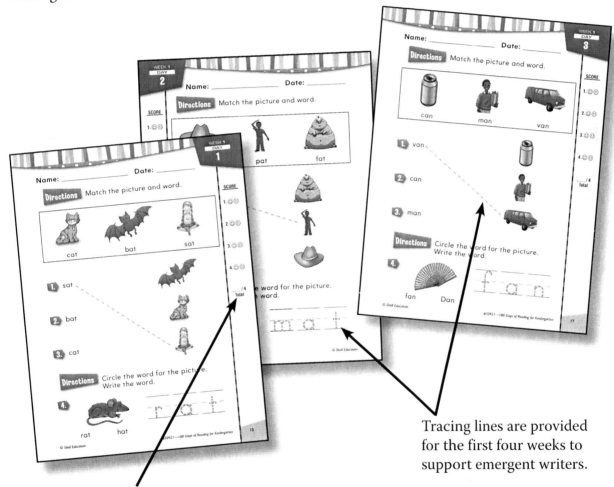

Tracing lines are provided for the first four weeks to support emergent writers.

Using the Scoring Guide

Use the scoring guide along the side of each practice page to check answers and see at a glance which skills may need more reinforcement.

Fill in the appropriate circle for each item to indicate correct (☺) or incorrect (☹) responses. You might wish to indicate only incorrect responses to focus on those skills. (For example, if students consistently miss items 2 and 4, they may need additional help with those concepts as outlined in the table on page 4.) Use the answer key at the back of the book to score the items, or you may call out answers to have students self-score or peer-score their work.

HOW TO USE THIS BOOK *(cont.)*

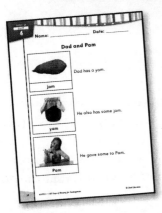  

An emergent-reader text is used for Day 4. Students answer comprehension questions on Day 4. This text can also be used for fluency practice (see page 7). Day 5 offers students the opportunity to complete a story and practice writing.

Writing Rubric

Score students' written response using the rubric below. Display the rubric for students to reference as they write (writingrubric.doc; writingrubric.pdf).

Points	Criteria
4	• Uses drawing, dictating, and writing to express ideas • Expresses multiple ideas on a topic • Includes specific details, i.e., colors or size • Spells with a letter to represent each sound, or in chunks of phonics patterns • Demonstrates an intended purpose in writing
3	• Uses drawing, dictating, and writing to express ideas • Expresses at least one idea on a topic • Spells with beginning and/or ending sounds
2	• Uses only drawing and dictating to express ideas • Attempts to express an idea on a topic • Attempts to spell with beginning and/or ending sounds
1	• Uses only drawing to express ideas • Does not convey an idea that relates to the topic
0	Offers no writing

   © Shell Education

HOW TO USE THIS BOOK *(cont.)*

Developing Students' Fluency Skills

What Is Fluency?

According to the National Reading Panel Report, there are five critical factors that are vital to effective reading instruction: phonemic awareness, phonics, fluency, vocabulary, and comprehension (2000). Rasinski (2006) defines fluency as "the ability to accurately and effortlessly decode the written words and then to give meaning to those words through appropriate phrasing and oral expression of the words." Wolf (2005) notes that the goal of developing fluency is comprehension rather than the ability to read rapidly. Becoming a fluent reader is a skill that develops gradually and requires practice. Reading text repeatedly with a different purpose each time supports the development of fluency in young children (Rasinski 2003).

At the kindergarten level, students can begin to develop early fluency skills. The emergent-reader texts provided in this book offer exposure to sight words and offer oral-reading opportunities to develop phonemic awareness.

Assessing Fluency

Fluent readers read accurately, with expression, and at a good pace. A Fluency Rubric along with detailed instructions for scoring and keeping oral reading records is included on the Digital Resource CD (fluency.pdf).

The table below lists fluency norms for grades 1–6 (Rasinski 2003):

Student Fluency Norms Based On Words Correct Per Minute (WCPM)			
Grade	Fall	Winter	Spring
1	—	—	60 wcpm
2	53	78	94
3	79	93	114
4	99	112	118
5	105	118	128
6	115	132	145

HOW TO USE THIS BOOK *(cont.)*

Diagnostic Assessment

Teachers can use the practice pages as diagnostic assessments. The data analysis tools included with the book enable teachers or parents to quickly score students' work and monitor their progress. Teachers and parents can see at a glance which reading concepts or skills students may need to target in order to develop proficiency.

After students complete a practice page, grade each page using the answer key (pages 231–242). Then, complete the Practice Page Item Analysis for the appropriate day (pages 10–11, or pageitem1.pdf and pageitem2.pdf) for the whole class, or the Student Item Analysis (pages 12–13, or studentitem1.pdf and studentitem2.pdf) for individual students. These charts are also provided as both Microsoft Word® files and as Microsoft Excel® files. Teachers can input data into the electronic files directly on the computer, or they can print the pages and analyze students' work using paper and pencil.

To complete the Practice Page Item Analyses:

- Write or type students' names in the far-left column. Depending on the number of students, more than one copy of the form may be needed, or you may need to add rows.

- The item numbers are included across the top of the charts. Each item correlates with the matching question number from the practice page.

- For each student, record an *X* in the column if the student has the item incorrect. If the item is correct, leave the item blank.

- If you are using the Excel file, totals will be automatically generated. If you are using the Word file or if you have printed the PDF, you will need to compute the totals. Count the *X*s in each row and column and fill in the correct boxes.

To complete the Student Item Analyses:

- Write or type the student's name on the top row. This form tracks the ongoing progress of each student, so one copy per student is necessary.

- The item numbers are included across the top of the chart. Each item correlates with the matching question number from the practice page.

- For each day, record an *X* in the column if the student has the item incorrect. If the item is correct, leave the item blank.

- If you are using the Excel file, totals will be automatically generated. If you are using the Word file or if you have printed the PDF, you will need to compute the totals. Count the *X*s in each row and column and fill in the correct boxes.

HOW TO USE THIS BOOK *(cont.)*

Using the Results to Differentiate Instruction

Once results are gathered and analyzed, teachers can use the results to inform the way they differentiate instruction. The data can help determine which concepts are the most difficult for students and which need additional instructional support and continued practice. Depending on how often the practice pages are scored, results can be considered for instructional support on a daily or weekly basis.

Whole-Class Support

The results of the diagnostic analysis may show that the entire class is struggling with a particular concept or group of concepts. If these concepts have been taught in the past, this indicates that further instruction or reteaching is necessary. If these concepts have not been taught in the past, this data is a great preassessment and demonstrates that students do not have a working knowledge of the concepts. Thus, careful planning for the length of the unit(s) or lesson(s) must be considered, and additional frontloading may be required.

Small-Group or Individual Support

The results of the diagnostic analysis may show that an individual or small group of students is struggling with a particular concept or group of concepts. If these concepts have been taught in the past, this indicates that further instruction or reteaching is necessary. Consider pulling aside these students while others are working independently to instruct further on the concept(s). Teachers can also use the results to help identify individuals or groups of proficient students who are ready for enrichment or above-grade-level instruction. These students may benefit from independent learning contracts or more challenging activities. Students may also benefit from extra practice using games or computer-based resources.

Digital Resource CD

The Digital Resource CD provides the following resources:

- Standards Correlations Chart

- Reproducible PDFs of each practice page

- Directions for completing the diagnostic Item Analysis forms

- Practice Page Item Analysis PDFs, Word documents, and Excel spreadsheets

- Student Item Analysis PDFs, Word documents, and Excel spreadsheets

- Fluency Assessment directions and rubric

PRACTICE PAGE ITEM ANALYSIS DAYS 1-3

Directions: Record an *X* in cells to indicate where students have missed questions. Add up the totals. You can view the following: (1) which items were missed per student; (2) the total correct score for each student; and (3) the total number of students who missed each item.

Week: _____ Day: _____

Student Name	Item # 1	2	3	4	# correct
Sample Student		X			3/4
# of students missing each question					

PRACTICE PAGE ITEM ANALYSIS DAYS 4-5

Directions: Record an X in cells to indicate where students have missed questions. Add up the totals. You can view the following: (1) which items were missed per student; (2) the total correct score for each student; and (3) the total number of students who missed each item.

Week: _____ Day: _____

Student Name	Item # 1	2	3	4	# correct	Written Response
Sample Student		X			3/4	3
# of students missing each question						

Written Response Average: _____

© Shell Education

STUDENT ITEM ANALYSIS DAYS 1-3

Directions: Record an *X* in cells to indicate where the student has missed questions. Add up the totals. You can view the following: (1) which items the student missed; (2) the total correct score per day; and (3) the total number of times each item was missed.

Student Name: **Sample Student**						
Item		1	2	3	4	# correct
Week	**Day**					
1	**1**		**X**			**3/4**
	Total					

© Shell Education

STUDENT ITEM ANALYSIS DAYS 4-5

Directions: Record an *X* in cells to indicate where the student has missed questions. Add up the totals. You can view the following: (1) which items the student missed; (2) the total correct score per day; and (3) the total number of times each item was missed.

Student Name: Sample Student						
	Day 4					Day 5
Item	1	2	3	4	# correct	Written Response
Week						
1		X			3/4	3
Total						
						Written Response Average:

STANDARDS CORRELATIONS

Shell Education is committed to producing educational materials that are research and standards based. In this effort, we have correlated all of our products to the academic standards of all 50 United States, the District of Columbia, the Department of Defense Dependent Schools, and all Canadian provinces.

How To Find Standards Correlations

To print a customized correlation report of this product for your state, visit our website at http://www.shelleducation.com and follow the on-screen directions. If you require assistance in printing correlation reports, please contact Customer Service at 1-877-777-3450.

Purpose and Intent of Standards

Legislation mandates that all states adopt academic standards that identify the skills students will learn in kindergarten through grade twelve. Many states also have standards for Pre-K. This same legislation sets requirements to ensure the standards are detailed and comprehensive.

Standards are designed to focus instruction and guide adoption of curricula. Standards are statements that describe the criteria necessary for students to meet specific academic goals. They define the knowledge, skills, and content students should acquire at each level. Standards are also used to develop standardized tests to evaluate students' academic progress. Teachers are required to demonstrate how their lessons meet state standards. State standards are used in the development of all of our products, so educators can be assured they meet the academic requirements of each state.

Common Core State Standards

The activities in this book are aligned to the Common Core State Standards (CCSS). The chart on page 4 and on the Digital Resource CD (standards.pdf) lists each standard that is addressed in this product.

TESOL and WIDA Standards

The activities in this book promote English language development for English language learners. The standards listed on the Digital Resource CD (standards.pdf) support the activities presented in this product.

Name: _____ **Date:** _____

Directions Match the words to the pictures.

cat   bat   sat

 1. sat

 2. bat

 3. cat

Directions Circle the word for the picture.
Write the word.

4.

rat   hat

Name: _____   Date: _____

SCORE

1. ☺ ☹

2. ☺ ☹

3. ☺ ☹

4. ☺ ☹

____ / 4
Total

Directions Match the words to the pictures.

hat   pat   fat

1. pat

2. hat

3. fat

Directions Circle the word for the picture.
Write the word.

4.

m a t

cat   mat

Name: _____ **Date:** _____

Directions Match the words to the pictures.

SCORE

1. ☺ ☹

2. ☺ ☹

3. ☺ ☹

4. ☺ ☹

____ / 4
Total

can   man   van

 **1.** van

2. can

3. man

Directions Circle the word for the picture.
Write the word.

4.

fan   Dan

Name: _____ Date: _____

The Bat and the Rat

A bat sat.

A rat sat.

A man sees them.

Oh no, a bat and a rat!

#50921—180 Days of Reading for Kindergarten   © Shell Education

Name: _____ **Date:** _____

Directions Listen to and read "The Bat and the Rat." Answer the questions.

---

1. Who sees the bat?

Ⓐ a cat

Ⓑ Dan

Ⓒ a man

3. Why is the man surprised?

Ⓐ He did not like the bat and rat.

Ⓑ He likes the bat and rat.

Ⓒ He did not like the mat.

2. What did the rat do?

Ⓐ ran

Ⓑ sat

Ⓒ jab

4. Which is another good title?

Ⓐ On the Mat

Ⓑ A Big Surprise

Ⓒ A Man

Name: _____   Date: _____

SCORE

____ / 4
Total

Directions   Look at the story. What happens next? Finish the story with a picture. Label the picture.

A bat sat.

The bat has a hat.

The rat sat.

_____

_ _

_____

#50921—180 Days of Reading for Kindergarten   © Shell Education

Name: _____ **Date:** _____

Directions Match the words to the pictures.

ham   yam   Pam

1. Pam

2. ham

3. yam

Directions Circle the word for the picture.
Write the word.

4.

jam   dam

Name: _____ Date: _____

SCORE

1. ☺ ☹

2. ☺ ☹

3. ☺ ☹

4. ☺ ☹

____ / 4
Total

Directions Match the words to the pictures.

bad　　　　Dad　　　　pad

1. Dad

2. pad

3. bad

Directions Circle the word for the picture.
Write the word.

4.

sad　　　had

Name: _____ **Date:** _____

SCORE

1. 😊 😐

2. 😊 😐

3. 😊 😐

4. 😊 😐

____ / 4
Total

Directions Match the words to the pictures.

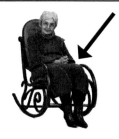  

lap   nap   map

1. map

2. lap

3. nap

Directions Circle the word for the picture.
Write the word.

4.

____ ____ ____

c a p

sap   cap

Name: _____ Date: _____

Dad and Pam

yam

Dad has a yam.

jam

He also has some jam.

Pam

He gave some to Pam.

#50921—180 Days of Reading for Kindergarten   © Shell Education

Name: _____ Date: _____

Directions Listen to and read "Dad and Pam."
Answer the questions.

SCORE

1. ☺ ☺

2. ☺ ☺

3. ☺ ☺

4. ☺ ☺

_____ / 4
Total

1. Who gave a gift?

Ⓐ Dad

Ⓑ Pam

Ⓒ yam

3. What will Pam do with the jam and yam?

Ⓐ sleep

Ⓑ eat them

Ⓒ sell them

2. What did Pam get?

Ⓐ naps

Ⓑ jam

Ⓒ Dad

4. Which is another good title?

Ⓐ Sharing

Ⓑ Yams

Ⓒ Naps

Name: _____   Date: _____

SCORE

___ / 4
Total

Directions   Look at the story. What happens next? Finish the story with a picture. Label the picture.

Pam is sad.   Pam is lost.   Pam has a map.

Name: _____ **Date:** _____

SCORE

Directions Match the words to the pictures.

can   cab   cap

1. ☺ ☹

2. ☺ ☹

3. ☺ ☹

4. ☺ ☹

____ / 4
Total

1. cab

2. can

3. cap

Directions Circle the word for the picture.
Write the word.

4.

cad   cat

____ ____ ____

c a t

Name: _____   Date: _____

SCORE

1. ☺ ☺

2. ☺ ☺

3. ☺ ☺

4. ☺ ☺

____ / 4
Total

Directions Match the words to the pictures.

mat   mad   man

1. man

2. mad

3. mat

Directions Circle the word for the picture.
Write the word.

4.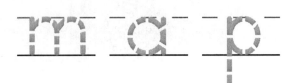

map   mag

Name: _____ **Date:** _____

Directions Match the words to the pictures.

SCORE

1. ☺ ☺

2. ☺ ☺

3. ☺ ☺

4. ☺ ☺

____ / 4
Total

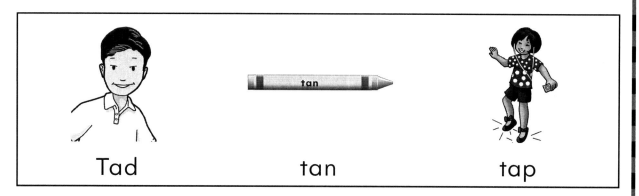

Tad   tan   tap

1. tap

2. tan

3. Tad

Directions Circle the word for the picture.
Write the word.

4.

tab   tag

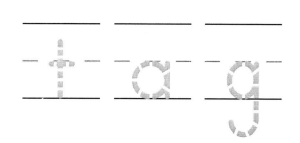

Name: _____ **Date:** _____

Zap

Zap had a nap.

Zap was on a mat.

Yap! Yap! Yap!

Zap got a bone.

Zap was glad.

© Shell Education

Name: _____ **Date:** _____

Directions Listen to and read "Zap." Answer the questions.

1. What was Zap on?

- Ⓐ a map
- Ⓑ a cat
- Ⓒ a mat

3. Why was Zap glad?

- Ⓐ He likes bones.
- Ⓑ He likes Dad.
- Ⓒ He likes to yap.

2. What did Zap get?

- Ⓐ a bed
- Ⓑ a bone
- Ⓒ a rag

4. Why did Zap get a bone?

- Ⓐ He began to yap.
- Ⓑ He got up.
- Ⓒ He got a bone.

1. ☺ ☹

2. ☺ ☹

3. ☺ ☹

4. ☺ ☹

_____ / 4
Total

SCORE

____ / 4
Total

Name: _____ **Date:** _____

Directions Look at the story. What happens next? Finish the story with a picture. Label the picture.

Sam has a can.

Sam trips on the mat.

Sam gets a rag.

_____

_____

#50921—180 Days of Reading for Kindergarten   © Shell Education

Name: _____ **Date:** _____

SCORE

Directions Match the words to the pictures.

jam   bag   dad

1. ☺ 😐

2. ☺ 😐

3. ☺ 😐

4. ☺ 😐

____ / 4
Total

1. bag

2. jam

3. Dad

Directions Circle the word for the picture.
Write the word.

4.

bad   wag

Name: _____   Date: _____

SCORE

1. ☺ ☺

2. ☺ ☺

3. ☺ ☺

4. ☺ ☺

____ / 4
Total

Directions Match the words to the pictures.

lab   cab   pan

1. pan

2. lab

3. cab

Directions Circle the word for the picture.
Write the word.

4.

v a n

van   had

Name: _____ **Date:** _____

Directions Match the words to the pictures.

ham   nap   bat

1. bat

2. ham

3. nap

Directions Circle the word for the picture.
Write the word.

4.

___ ___ ___

r a t

tap   rat

Name: _____ **Date:** _____

Dan's Ham

ham

Dan had a ham.

pan

He put it in a pan.

hot

The pan got hot.

stop

Stop!

© Shell Education

Name: _____ Date: _____

Directions Listen to and read "Dan's Ham." Answer the questions.

1. What did Dan have?

Ⓐ a yam

Ⓑ some jam

Ⓒ a ham

3. Why does Dan have to stop?

Ⓐ The ham got hot.

Ⓑ The pan got hot.

Ⓒ Sam was hot.

2. Where did Dan put the ham?

Ⓐ in a pot

Ⓑ in a pan

Ⓒ in a cup

4. Which is another good title?

Ⓐ Too Hot

Ⓑ Sam

Ⓒ Food

Name: _____   Date: _____

SCORE

___ / 4
Total

Directions   Look at the story. What happens next? Finish the story with a picture. Label the picture.

Pam sees
1 bat.

Pam sees
2 bats.

Pam sees
3 bats.

Name: _____ **Date:** _____

Directions Match the words to the pictures.

pig   wig   big

1. ☺ ☹

2. ☺ ☹

 1. wig

3. ☺ ☹

4. ☺ ☹

2. big

____ / 4
Total

 3. pig

Directions Circle the word for the picture. Write the word.

 4.

_____ _____ _____

_ _ _ _ _ _ _

_____ _____ _____

dig   fig

Name: _____   **Date:** _____

SCORE

1. ☺ ☹

2. ☺ ☹

3. ☺ ☹

4. ☺ ☹

___/ 4
Total

Directions Match the words to the pictures.

hit   bit   sit

1. sit

2. bit

3. hit

Directions Circle the word for the picture.
Write the word.

4.

lit   bit

_____ _____ _____

_ _ _ _ _ _ _ _ _

_____ _____ _____

Name: _____ **Date:** _____

Directions Match the words to the pictures.

win   pin   bin

1. ☺ ☺

1. bin

2. ☺ ☺

3. ☺ ☺

2. win

4. ☺ ☺

3. pin

____ / 4
Total

Directions Circle the word for the picture.
Write the word.

 4.

_____ _____ _____

_ _ _ _ _ _ _ _

_____ _____ _____

fin   tin

Name: _____   Date: _____

Jim and the Pig

Jim had a fit.

He bit a pig.

Quit it, Jim! Sit!

Tim will fix your food.

Name: _____ **Date:** _____

Directions Listen to and read "Jim and the Pig."
Answer the questions.

SCORE

1. ☺ ☹

2. ☺ ☹

3. ☺ ☹

4. ☺ ☹

____ / 4
Total

1. Who had a fit?

(A) Jim

(B) Tad

(C) Pip

3. Why do you think Jim had a fit?

(A) He wanted food.

(B) He wanted the pig.

(C) He wanted Tim to sit.

2. What did Tim tell Jim to do?

(A) go

(B) sit

(C) rip

4. Which is another good title?

(A) Tim

(B) Fix Food

(C) Calm Down!

Name: _____   Date: _____

SCORE

____ / 4
Total

Directions Look at the story. What happens next? Finish the story with a picture. Label the picture.

A kid can see a ball.

A kid can hit a ball.

A kid can see a ball.

Name: _____ **Date:** _____

Directions Match the words to the pictures.

SCORE

1. ☺ 😐

2. ☺ 😐

3. ☺ 😐

4. ☺ 😐

____ / 4
Total

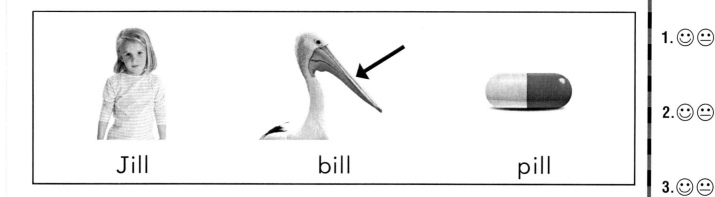

Jill   bill   pill

1. bill

2. pill

3. Jill

Directions Circle the word for the picture.
Write the word.

4.

_____ _____

- - - - - - - - - - - - - - - - -

_____

hill   sill

Name: _____ **Date:** _____

SCORE

1. ☺ ☹

2. ☺ ☹

3. ☺ ☹

4. ☺ ☹

___ / 4
Total

Directions Match the words to the pictures.

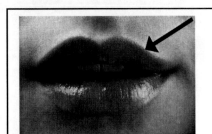  

lip   rip   hip

1. hip

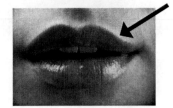

2. rip

3. lip

Directions Circle the word for the picture.
Write the word.

4.

___ ___ ___

– – – – – – – – –

___ ___ ___

tip   zip

Name: _____ **Date:** _____

Directions Match the words to the pictures.

kick   pick   sick

1. sick

2. kick

3. pick

Directions Circle the word for the picture.
Write the word.

4.

_____ _____ _____ _____

– – – – – – – – – – – – – – – – –

_____ _____ _____

tick   lick

Name: _____ Date: _____

Jill Plays Soccer

Jill

Jill kicks a ball.

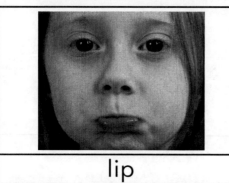
lip

It hits her in the lip.

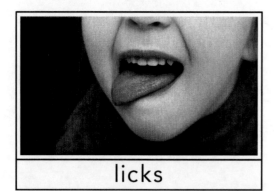
licks

She licks her lip.

kicks

Then she kicks the ball again.

    #50921—180 Days of Reading for Kindergarten   © Shell Education

Name: _____ Date: _____

Directions Listen to and read "Jill Plays Soccer." Answer the questions.

1. Who kicked the ball?

Ⓐ soccer ball

Ⓑ Jill

Ⓒ lip

3. Why did Jill lick her lip?

Ⓐ She kicked a soccer ball.

Ⓑ She kicked the ball again.

Ⓒ The ball hit her lip.

2. What did the ball hit?

Ⓐ Jill's lip

Ⓑ the soccer ball

Ⓒ lick

4. What does this text tell?

Ⓐ Jill hurt herself with the soccer ball.

Ⓑ Soccer is fun.

Ⓒ Games are fun.

SCORE

___ / 4
Total

Name: _____ Date: _____

Directions Look at the story. What happens next? Finish the story with a picture. Label the picture.

Jill trips
on a mitt.

Jill rips
her shirt.

Jill gets
a pin.

_____

- -

_____

WEEK 7
DAY
1

Name: _____ **Date:** _____

Directions Match the words to the pictures.

hit　　　　　him　　　　　hid

1. ☺ 😐

2. ☺ 😐

3. ☺ 😐

4. ☺ 😐

1. hid

2. him

3. hit

____ / 4
Total

Directions Circle the word for the picture.
Write the word.

4.

_____ _____ _____

- - - - - - -

_____ _____ _____

hip　　　hid

© Shell Education #50921—180 Days of Reading for Kindergarten　51

Name: _____   **Date:** _____

SCORE

1. ☺ ☻

2. ☺ ☻

3. ☺ ☻

4. ☺ ☻

_____ / 4
Total

Directions Match the words to the pictures.

pick   pill   pit

1. pick

2. pit

3. pill

Directions Circle the word for the picture.
Write the word.

4.

_____ _____ _____

- - - - - - - - - - - - - - - - - -

_____ _____ _____

pit   pin

Name: _____ **Date:** _____

Directions Match the words to the pictures.

SCORE

1. ☺ ☺
2. ☺ ☺
3. ☺ ☺
4. ☺ ☺

___ / 4
Total

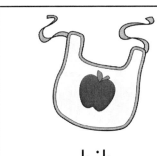  

bib　　　　big　　　　bit

 1. bit

 2. bib

3. big

Directions Circle the word for the picture. Write the word.

 4.

_____ _____ _____

— — — — — — — —

_____ _____ _____

bin　　　bid

Name: _____ Date: _____

Pib Likes to Dig

Pib likes to dig.

He digs in the bin.

Get him out of the bin!

Kim puts Pib in the sink.

Meow!

#50921—180 Days of Reading for Kindergarten
© Shell Education

Name: _____ **Date:** _____

Directions Listen to and read "Pib Likes to Dig."
Answer the questions.

SCORE

1. ☺ ☺

2. ☺ ☺

3. ☺ ☺

4. ☺ ☺

____ / 4
Total

1. Who likes to dig?

(A) Pib

(B) Kim

(C) the bin

3. Why does Kim put Pib in the sink?

(A) Pib got dirty.

(B) Pib likes the sink.

(C) Pib wants to dig.

2. Where does Pib dig?

(A) out of the bin

(B) in the bin

(C) with Kim

4. Which is another good title?

(A) Cat

(B) Messy Pib

(C) Kim's Job

Name: _____   Date: _____

SCORE

___ / 4
Total

Directions Look at the story. What happens next? Finish the story with a picture. Label the picture.

Pip has a bib.   Pip bit.   It has a pit.

Name: _____ **Date:** _____

Directions Match the words to the pictures.

 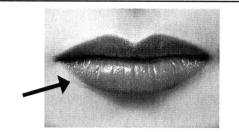 

Kim   lip   hit

SCORE

1. ☺ ☺

2. ☺ ☺

3. ☺ ☺

4. ☺ ☺

____ / 4
Total

1. hit

2. lip

3. Kim

Directions Circle the word for the picture.
Write the word.

4.    _____ _____ _____

          _ _ _ _ _ _ _ _ _ _

          _____ _____ _____

jig   lid

Name: _____ **Date:** _____

SCORE

1. ☺ ☺

2. ☺ ☺

3. ☺ ☺

4. ☺ ☺

____ / 4
Total

Directions Match the words to the pictures.

6

six   dig   rip

6

1. rip

2. dig

3. six

Directions Circle the word for the picture.
Write the word.

4.

_____ _____ _____ _____

- - - - - - - - - - - -

_____ _____ _____ _____

pill   pits

Name: _____ **Date:** _____

Directions Match the words to the pictures.

SCORE

fig   bib   kid

1. ☺ 😐

2. ☺ 😐

3. ☺ 😐

4. ☺ 😐

____ / 4
Total

1. kid

2. bib

3. fig

Directions Circle the word for the picture.
Write the word.

4.

____ ____ ____ ____

sick   wins

Name: _____ **Date:** _____

Kim Gets Sick

sick

It's not fun to be sick.

Kim

Kim will need a nap.

pill

Kim may need a pill.

Get well quick!

     © *Shell Education*

Name: _____ **Date:** _____

Directions Listen to and read "Kim Gets Sick."
Answer the questions.

SCORE

1. ☺ ☹

2. ☺ ☺

3. ☺ ☹

4. ☺ ☹

____ / 4
Total

1. Who is sick?

Ⓐ a pill

Ⓑ Kim

Ⓒ Tim

3. Why is it not fun to be sick?

Ⓐ You may feel bad.

Ⓑ You may feel good.

Ⓒ You may feel well.

2. What may Kim need?

Ⓐ a pill

Ⓑ to be sick

Ⓒ to have fun

4. Which is another good title?

Ⓐ Tim

Ⓑ A Pill

Ⓒ Get Well

SCORE

___ / 4
Total

Name: _____ Date: _____

Directions Look at the story. What happens next? Finish the story with a picture. Label the picture.

Kim sits.

Rick sits.

Kim digs.

#50921—180 Days of Reading for Kindergarten   © Shell Education

Name: _____ **Date:** _____

Directions Match the words to the pictures.

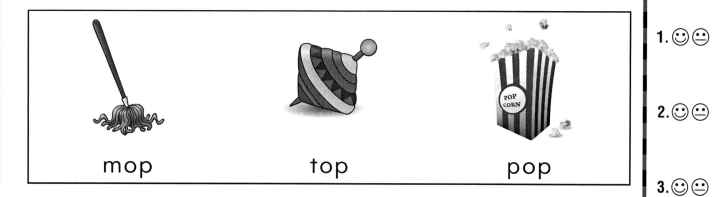

mop　　　　　　top　　　　　　pop

1. top

2. mop

3. pop

Directions Circle the word for the picture.
Write the word.

4.

_____ _____ _____

- - - - - - - - -

_____ _____ _____

cop　　　　hop

Name: _____ Date: _____

SCORE

1. ☺ ☹

2. ☺ ☹

3. ☺ ☹

4. ☺ ☹

_____ / 4
Total

Directions Match the words to the pictures.

cot   dot   hot

1. hot

2. cot

3. dot

Directions Circle the word for the picture.
Write the word.

4.

_____ _____ _____

- - - - - - -

_____ _____ _____

lot   pot

Name: _____ Date: _____

Directions Match the words to the pictures.

dog

hog

jog

1. jog

2. hog

3. dog

Directions Circle the word for the picture.
Write the word.

4.

_____ _____ _____

‑ ‑ ‑ ‑ ‑ ‑

_____ _____ _____

log   fog

Name: _____ Date: _____

Bob's Hot Pot

Bob got a pot hot.

He put in corn on the cob.

He did not put on a top.

Bob got a mop.

 #50921—180 Days of Reading for Kindergarten © Shell Education

Name: _____ **Date:** _____

Directions Listen to and read "Bob's Hot Pot."
Answer the questions.

SCORE

1. ☺ ☹

2. ☺ ☹

3. ☺ ☹

4. ☺ ☹

____ / 4
Total

1. What did Bob put in the pot?

Ⓐ a hot top

Ⓑ a hot sock

Ⓒ corn on the cob

3. What did Bob do to the pot?

Ⓐ got a top

Ⓑ got it hot

Ⓒ got a mop

2. What did Bob **not** do?

Ⓐ put on a top

Ⓑ put in the corn

Ⓒ get the pot hot

4. What was Bob's job?

Ⓐ to mop up

Ⓑ to cook corn

Ⓒ to get a top

Name: _____ Date: _____

Directions Look at the story. What happens next? Finish the story with a picture. Label the picture.

Don got
a pot.

Don got
popcorn.

The corn
can pop.

Name: _____ **Date:** _____

Directions Match the words to the pictures.

dot   Don   dock

1. Don

2. dot

3. dock

Directions Circle the word for the picture.
Write the word.

4.  ____ ____ ____

- - - - - - - - - -

____ ____ ____

dot   dog

Name: _____ Date: _____

SCORE

1. ☺ ☹

2. ☺ ☹

3. ☺ ☹

4. ☺ ☹

____ / 4
Total

Directions Match the words to the pictures.

cop   cob   cost

1. cost

2. cop

3. cob

Directions Circle the word for the picture.
Write the word.

4.

_____ _____ _____

\- \- \- \- \- \- \- \- \-

_____ _____ _____

cot   con

Name: _____ **Date:** _____

SCORE

Directions Match the words to the pictures.

hot   hog   honk

1. ☺ 😐

2. ☺ 😐

3. ☺ 😐

4. ☺ 😐

____ / 4
Total

1. honk

2. hot

3. hog

Directions Circle the word for the picture.
Write the word.

4.    _____ _____ _____

    _ _ _ _ _ _ _ _ _ _

    _____ _____ _____

hop   hot

Name: _____ **Date:** _____

Mom Shops

Mom

Mom went to the shop.

clock

She got a clock for Bob.

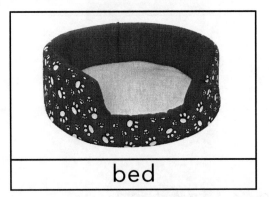
bed

She got a bed for the dog.

What did she get for herself?

Name: _____ **Date:** _____

Directions Listen to and read "Mom Shops."
Answer the questions.

1. Who bought
the gifts?

Ⓐ Mom

Ⓑ Bob

Ⓒ dog

3. What did Mom buy
for herself?

Ⓐ a clock

Ⓑ flowers

Ⓒ a bed

2. Where did Mom go?

Ⓐ the clock

Ⓑ the shop

Ⓒ to bed

4. Which is another
good title?

Ⓐ Gifts

Ⓑ Shops

Ⓒ Clocks

Name: _____   Date: _____

SCORE

___ / 4
Total

Directions Look at the story. What happens next? Finish the story with a picture. Label the picture.

Hoff has corn on the cob.

Hoff likes corn on the cob.

The dog does not.

_____

_ _

_____

Name: _____ **Date:** _____

SCORE

1. ☺ ☹

2. ☺ ☹

3. ☺ ☹

4. ☺ ☹

____ / 4
Total

Directions Match the words to the pictures.

rod   mop   box

1. box

2. mop

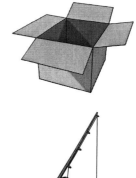

3. rod

Directions Circle the word for the picture. Write the word.

4.

_____ _____ _____

_ _ _ _ _ _ _ _ _ _ _

_____ _____ _____

hot   hog

Name: _____ **Date:** _____

SCORE

1. ☺ ☺

2. ☺ ☺

3. ☺ ☺

4. ☺ ☺

_____ / 4
Total

Directions Match the words to the pictures.

dot   lock   dog

1. dog

2. lock

3. dot

Directions Circle the word for the picture.
Write the word.

4.

_____ _____ _____
_ _ _ _ _ _ _
_____ _____ _____

fox   got

#50921—180 Days of Reading for Kindergarten   © Shell Education

Name: _____ **Date:** _____

Directions Match the words to the pictures.

jog

pop

Mom

1. pop

2. jog

3. Mom

Directions Circle the word for the picture.
Write the word.

4.

_____ _____ _____

— — — — — — — —

_____ _____ _____

rot   log

Name: _____ Date: _____

Naps

A dog can nap in a box.

A fox can nap in a den.

A frog can nap on a log.

A hog can nap in a pen.

#50921—180 Days of Reading for Kindergarten

© Shell Education

Name: _____ **Date:** _____

Directions Listen to and read "Naps." Answer the questions.

1. Where can a dog nap?

Ⓐ in a den

Ⓑ in a box

Ⓒ in a pen

3. Where can you nap?

Ⓐ in a bed

Ⓑ in a fox den

Ⓒ in a hog pen

2. Where can a fox nap?

Ⓐ in a den

Ⓑ in a box

Ⓒ on a log

4. Which is another good title?

Ⓐ Bedtime

Ⓑ Animals

Ⓒ Logs and Pens

SCORE

____ / 4
Total

Name: _____   Date: _____

Directions Look at the story. What happens next? Finish the story with a picture. Label the picture.

Mom has a box.

Mom opens the box.

#50921—180 Days of Reading for Kindergarten   © Shell Education

Name: _____ **Date:** _____

Directions Match the words to the pictures.

hen   pen   men

1. men

2. pen

3. hen

Directions Circle the word for the picture.
Write the word.

4.

10

Len   ten

_____ _____ _____

- - - - - - - - -

_____ _____ _____

Name: _____   Date: _____

SCORE

1. ☺ ☻

2. ☺ ☻

3. ☺ ☻

4. ☺ ☻

_____ / 4
Total

Directions Match the words to the pictures.

  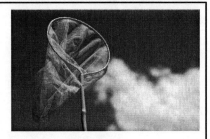

jet   pet   net

1. net

2. pet

3. jet

Directions Circle the word for the picture.
Write the word.

4.

wet   set

_____ _____ _____
_ _ _ _ _ _ _
_____ _____ _____

#50921—180 Days of Reading for Kindergarten   © Shell Education

Name: _____ **Date:** _____

Directions Match the words to the pictures.

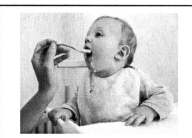  

fed   red   Ned

1. ☺ ☺

2. ☺ ☺

3. ☺ ☺

4. ☺ ☺

1. Ned

2. red

____ / 4
Total

3. fed

Directions Circle the word for the picture.
Write the word.

4.

____ ____ ____

- - - - - -

____ ____ ____

led   bed

Name: _____ Date: _____

Ted and his Hen

hen

Ted has a hen.

eggs

He sells the eggs.

money

Ted gets money to spend.

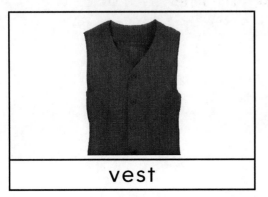

vest

He wants a red vest.

© Shell Education

Name: _____ Date: _____

Directions Listen to and read "Ted and his Hen."
Answer the questions.

1. Where does Ted get eggs from?

Ⓐ a farm

Ⓑ his hen

Ⓒ a shop

3. Why does Ted want to sell more eggs?

Ⓐ to get the red dress

Ⓑ to get a red vest

Ⓒ to get a red hat

2. What does Ted do with the eggs?

Ⓐ sells them

Ⓑ puts them in a store

Ⓒ gives them away

4. What does Ted get for the eggs?

Ⓐ a nest

Ⓑ a dress

Ⓒ money

Name: _____ Date: _____

SCORE

____ / 4
Total

Directions Look at the story. What happens next? Finish the story with a picture. Label the picture.

Fred gets a pan.

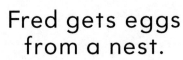

Fred gets eggs from a nest.

Fred gets pecked.

_____

_ _ _ _ _ _ _ _ _ _ _ _ _ _ _ _ _ _ _

_____

Name: _____ **Date:** _____

Directions Match the words to the pictures.

peg   beg   Meg

1. beg

2. peg

3. Meg

Directions Circle the word for the picture.
Write the word.

4.

____ ____ ____

– – – – – – – – –

____ ____ ____

leg   peg

Name: _____ Date: _____

SCORE

1. ☺ ☺

2. ☺ ☺

3. ☺ ☺

4. ☺ ☺

_____ / 4
Total

Directions Match the words to the pictures.

bell   fell   yell

1. yell

2. bell

3. fell

Directions Circle the word for the picture.
Write the word.

4.

___ ___ ___ ___

_ _ _ _ _ _

___ ___ ___ ___

well   Nell

Name: _____   Date: _____

Directions Match the words to the pictures.

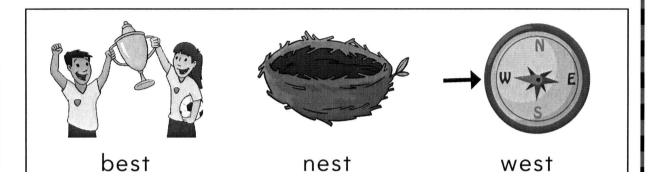

best   nest   west

1. west

2. nest

3. best

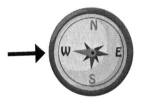

Directions Circle the word for the picture.
Write the word.

4.

——— ——— ——— ———

— — — — — — — —

——— ——— ——— ———

test   vest

Name: _____ Date: _____

Meg Gets to Fish

Meg went to the tent.

She put on a vest.

She got her net.

She did her best to get fish!

#50921—180 Days of Reading for Kindergarten   © Shell Education

Name: _____ **Date:** _____

Directions Listen to and read "Meg Gets to Fish." Answer the questions.

SCORE

1. ☺ ☺

2. ☺ ☺

3. ☺ ☺

4. ☺ ☺

____ / 4
Total

1. Who will go fishing?

(A) Meg

(B) the net

(C) the tent

2. Where is Meg?

(A) at home

(B) in a tent

(C) at school

3. How will Meg get the fish?

(A) with her vest

(B) with the net

(C) with her hands

4. Which is another good title?

(A) Wearing a Vest

(B) Has a Net

(C) Set to Fish

Name: _____ **Date:** _____

SCORE

____ / 4
Total

Directions Look at the story. What happens next? Finish the story with a picture. Label the picture.

Nell sees
a well.

Nell goes
to the well.

Nell lets
down the pail.

_____

- -

_____

      © Shell Education

Name: _____ **Date:** _____

Directions Match the words to the pictures.

pet   peg   pest

1. ☺ ☹

2. ☺ ☹

3. ☺ ☹

4. ☺ ☹

1. pest   

2. peg   

____ / 4
Total

3. pet   

Directions Circle the word for the picture.
Write the word.

4.

____ ____ ____

_ _ _ _ _ _ _ _ _

____ ____ ____

pet   pen

© Shell Education

Name: _____ Date: _____

SCORE

1. ☺ ☺

2. ☺ ☺

3. ☺ ☺

4. ☺ ☺

___ / 4
Total

Directions Match the words to the pictures.

bed   Ben   bell

1. bell

2. Ben

3. bed

Directions Circle the word for the picture.
Write the word.

4.

___ ___ ___

‑ ‑ ‑ ‑ ‑ ‑ ‑

___ ___ ___

beg   best

Name: _____ **Date:** _____

Directions Match the words to the pictures.

well   wet   wed

1. ☺ ☺

2. ☺ ☺

3. ☺ ☺

1. wet

4. ☺ ☺

____ / 4
Total

2. wed

3. well

Directions Circle the word for the picture.
Write the word.

4.

web   when

_____ _____ _____

_ _ _ _ _ _ _ _ _ _ _ _ _ _ _

_____ _____ _____

Name: _____ Date: _____

Ben the Vet

vet

Ben is a vet.

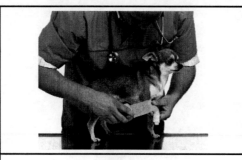

pet

A vet can help a pet.

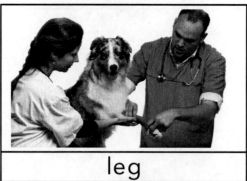

leg

Ben can fix a hurt leg.

Your pet will get well soon.

Name: _____   **Date:** _____

Directions Listen to and read "Ben the Vet."
Answer the questions.

SCORE

1. Who can help a sick pet?

(A) a vet

(B) a dad

(C) a kid

3. What is best about a vet?

(A) A vet gives shots.

(B) A vet helps pets.

(C) A vet gets well too.

2. What can a vet do to help?

(A) get on the bed

(B) fix a hurt leg

(C) make a mess

4. What is a vet?

(A) a doctor for kids

(B) a doctor for moms and dads

(C) a doctor for pets

1. ☺ ☹

2. ☺ ☹

3. ☺ ☹

4. ☺ ☹

____ / 4
Total

SCORE

___ / 4
Total

Name: _____   Date: _____

Directions Look at the story. What happens next? Finish the story with a picture. Label the picture.

Ed fed his pet.

Ed let it get wet.

Then Ed let it get out.

Name: _____ **Date:** _____

Directions Match the words to the pictures.

SCORE

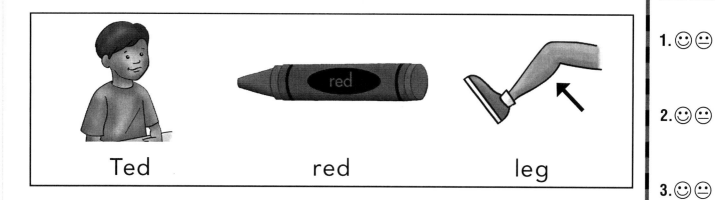

Ted   red   leg

1. leg
2. red
3. Ted

1. ☺ ☺
2. ☺ ☺
3. ☺ ☺
4. ☺ ☺

____ / 4
Total

Directions Circle the word for the picture.
Write the word.

4.

_____ _____ _____

– – – – – – – – – – –

_____ _____ _____

vet   hen

Name: _____ Date: _____

SCORE

1. ☺ ☹

2. ☺ ☹

3. ☺ ☹

4. ☺ ☹

_____ / 4
Total

Directions Match the words to the pictures.

Meg   pen   wet

1. wet

2. Meg

3. pen

Directions Circle the word for the picture.
Write the word.

4.    _____ _____ _____

                                 _ _ _ _ _ _ _ _ _

                                 _____ _____ _____

jet   web

Name: _____ **Date:** _____

Directions Match the words to the pictures.

SCORE

Ken vet ten

1. ☺ ☺

2. ☺ ☺

1. ten

3. ☺ ☺

4. ☺ ☺

2. vet

____ / 4
Total

3. Ken

Directions Circle the word for the picture.
Write the word.

4.  ____ ____ ____

‑ ‑ ‑ ‑ ‑ ‑

____ ____ ____

bed   pep

Name: _____ **Date:** _____

A Hen

This is a hen.

The baby is a chick.

They live in a pen.

They peck for seeds and corn.

#50921—*180 Days of Reading for Kindergarten* © *Shell Education*

Name: _____ **Date:** _____

Directions Listen to and read "A Hen." Answer the questions.

SCORE

1. ☺ ☺

2. ☺ ☺

3. ☺ ☺

4. ☺ ☺

____ / 4
Total

1. What is the baby called?

Ⓐ a chicken

Ⓑ a kid

Ⓒ a chick

3. Why do hens like seeds and corn?

Ⓐ They are in the dirt.

Ⓑ They are good to eat.

Ⓒ They are little.

2. Where do the hens live?

Ⓐ in a box

Ⓑ in the dirt

Ⓒ in a pen

4. What is this story about?

Ⓐ pens

Ⓑ hens

Ⓒ seeds and corn

Name: _____ **Date:** _____

SCORE

____ / 4
Total

Directions Look at the story. What happens next? Finish the story with a picture. Label the picture.

A hen lays eggs in a nest.

The hen sits on the eggs.

The hen hears *peck, peck, peck.*

Name: _____ **Date:** _____

Directions Match the words to the pictures.

jug   rug   dug

1. ☺ ☺

2. ☺ ☺

3. ☺ ☺

1. dug

4. ☺ ☺

2. rug

____ / 4
Total

3. jug

Directions Circle the word for the picture.
Write the word.

4.

_____ _____ _____

- - - - - - - - - - - -

_____ _____ _____

bug   hug

Name: _____ Date: _____

SCORE

1. ☺ ☹

2. ☺ ☹

3. ☺ ☹

4. ☺ ☹

_____ / 4
Total

Directions Match the words to the pictures.

cub   sub   rub

1. sub

2. rub

3. cub

Directions Circle the word for the picture.
Write the word.

4.    ____ ____ ____

                                   ‑ ‑ ‑ ‑ ‑

                                   ____ ____ ____

hub   tub

Name: _____ **Date:** _____

Directions Match the words to the pictures.

bun   fun   run

 run

 bun

 fun

Directions Circle the word for the picture.
Write the word.

4.

_____ _____ _____

_ _ _ _ _ _ _ _

_____ _____

sun   pun

Name: _____ Date: _____

Pups and Cubs

pup

A pup is a baby dog.

bat

A pup is a baby bat, too.

cub

A cub is a baby bear.

fox

A cub is a baby fox, too.

#50921—180 Days of Reading for Kindergarten
© Shell Education

Name: _____ Date: _____

SCORE

Directions Listen to and read "Pups and Cubs." Answer the questions.

1. What is a pup?

Ⓐ a baby bear

Ⓑ a baby dog

Ⓒ a baby bird

3. Which would make a good pet?

Ⓐ a gull

Ⓑ a cub

Ⓒ a pup

2. What is a cub?

Ⓐ a baby bear

Ⓑ a baby dog

Ⓒ a bug

4. Which is another good title?

Ⓐ Dogs

Ⓑ Bears

Ⓒ Baby Animals

1. ☺ ☺

2. ☺ ☺

3. ☺ ☺

4. ☺ ☺

____ / 4
Total

Name: _____ **Date:** _____

SCORE

___/ 4
Total

Directions Look at the story. What happens next? Finish the story with a picture. Label the picture.

A cub digs for grubs.

A pup runs for fun.

The cub and pup bump!

Name: _____ **Date:** _____

SCORE

Directions Match the words to the pictures.

cup   cud   cub

1. ☺ 😐

2. ☺ 😐

3. ☺ 😐

4. ☺ 😐

1. cup

2. cub

3. cud

___ / 4
Total

Directions Circle the word for the picture.
Write the word.

4. 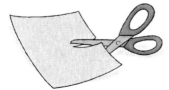   _____ _____ _____

_ _ _ _ _ _ _ _ _

_____ _____ _____

cup   cut

Name: _____   Date: _____

SCORE

1. ☺ ☹

2. ☺ ☹

3. ☺ ☹

4. ☺ ☹

____ / 4
Total

Directions Match the words to the pictures.

hug   huff   hum

1. huff

2. hum

3. hug

Directions Circle the word for the picture.
Write the word.

4.

hull   hut

____ ____ ____

- - - - - - - -

____ ____

#50921—180 Days of Reading for Kindergarten   © Shell Education

Name: _____ **Date:** _____

SCORE

Directions Match the words to the pictures.

run   ruff   rub

1. ☺ 😐

2. ☺ 😐

3. ☺ 😐

4. ☺ 😐

____ / 4
Total

1. ruff

2. rub

3. run

Directions Circle the word for the picture.
Write the word.

4.    _____ _____ _____

— — — — — — — — —

_____ _____ _____

rug   rust

Name: _____ **Date:** _____

Gus and His Pets

Gus has two pets.

Gus can run and jump with one pet.

Ruff! Ruff!

One pet does not run or jump.

Quack! Quack!

  #50921—180 Days of Reading for Kindergarten © Shell Education

Name: _____   **Date:** _____

Directions Listen to and read "Gus and His Pets." Answer the questions.

SCORE

1. ☺ ☹

2. ☺ ☹

3. ☺ ☹

4. ☺ ☹

____ / 4
Total

1. Who has pets?

Ⓐ a pup
Ⓑ a duck
Ⓒ Gus

3. What kinds of pets does Gus have?

Ⓐ a pup and a duck
Ⓑ a bug and pup
Ⓒ a duck and a cat

2. Which pet runs?

Ⓐ a pup
Ⓑ a duck
Ⓒ a bug

4. Which is another good title?

Ⓐ Duck in the Pond
Ⓑ Two Pets
Ⓒ Gus Runs

Name: _____   Date: _____

SCORE

_____ / 4
Total

Directions Look at the story. What happens next? Finish the story with a picture. Label the picture.

Rud fills
the tub.

Rud jumps
in the tub.

The pup jumps
in the tub.

_____

- -

_____

Name: _____ **Date:** _____

Directions Match the words to the pictures.

mug   hut   tug

1. hut

2. mug

3. tug

Directions Circle the word for the picture.
Write the word.

4.

_____ _____ _____

— — — — — — —

_____ _____ _____

cup   nut

Name: _____ **Date:** _____

SCORE

1. ☺ ☹

2. ☺ ☹

3. ☺ ☹

4. ☺ ☹

____ / 4
Total

Directions Match the words to the pictures.

gum   pup   nut

1. nut

2. pup

3. gum

Directions Circle the word for the picture.
Write the word.

4.

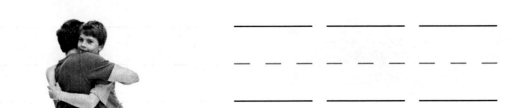

hug   puff

_____ _____ _____

- - - - - - - - - - - - - - - - - -

_____ _____ _____

Name: _____ Date: _____

SCORE

Directions Match the words to the pictures.

cut   Gus   rug

1. ☺ ☺

2. ☺ ☺

3. ☺ ☺

4. ☺ ☺

___ / 4
Total

1. rug

2. Gus

3. cut

Directions Circle the word for the picture.
Write the word.

4.

____ ____ ____

– – – – – – – –

____ ____ ____

sun   bus

© Shell Education   #50921—180 Days of Reading for Kindergarten   119

Name: _____ **Date:** _____

Bud Needs a Hug

Bud

Bud was glum.

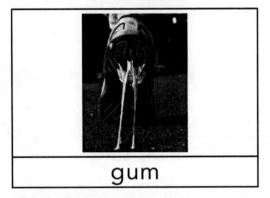

gum

His shoe got stuck in gum.

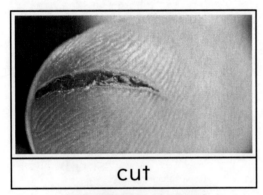

cut

He got a cut.

hug

You just need a hug, Bud!

© Shell Education

Name: _____ **Date:** _____

Directions Listen to and read "Bud Needs a Hug." Answer the questions.

1. Who got a cut?

Ⓐ Bud

Ⓑ the shoe

Ⓒ the gum

3. What does *glum* mean?

Ⓐ happy

Ⓑ sad

Ⓒ fun

2. What got on his shoe?

Ⓐ mud

Ⓑ mush

Ⓒ gum

4. Why did Bud need a hug?

Ⓐ because he was sad

Ⓑ because he got in the mud

Ⓒ because he lost his pup

1. ☺ ☹

2. ☺ ☹

3. ☺ ☹

4. ☺ ☹

___ / 4
Total

Name: _____ **Date:** _____

Directions Look at the story. What happens next? Finish the story with a picture. Label the picture.

Gus digs
in the mud.

Gus jumps
in a puddle.

Gus scuffs his
shoes on a rug.

Name: _____ **Date:** _____

Directions Match the words to the pictures.

SCORE

hat   hit   hot

1. ☺ ☻

2. ☺ ☻

3. ☺ ☻

1. hot

4. ☺ ☻

2. hit

____/ 4
Total

3. hat

Directions Circle the word for the picture.
Write the word.

4.

____ ____ ____

‒ ‒ ‒ ‒ ‒ ‒ ‒ ‒

____ ____ ____

hut   hat

Name: _____ Date: _____

SCORE

1. ☺ ☺

2. ☺ ☺

3. ☺ ☺

4. ☺ ☺

____ / 4
Total

Directions Match the words to the pictures.

pot   pit   pat

1. pat

2. pit

3. pot

Directions Circle the word for the picture.
Write the word.

4.

_____ _____ _____

- - - - - - - - -

_____ _____ _____

pet   put

  #50921—180 Days of Reading for Kindergarten © Shell Education

Name: _____ **Date:** _____

Directions Match the words to the pictures.

bag   big   beg

1. ☺ ☺

2. ☺ ☺

3. ☺ ☺

4. ☺ ☺

____ / 4
Total

1. beg

2. bag

3. big

Directions Circle the word for the picture.
Write the word.

4.

____ ____ ____

‐ ‐ ‐ ‐ ‐ ‐

____ ____ ____

bug   bog

Name: _____   Date: _____

The Hot Hut

Sid is sad.

It is hot in the hut.

The cat is near the cot.

The dog is on the mat.

Name: _____   Date: _____

Directions Listen to and read "The Hot Hut." Answer the questions.

1. Who is sad?

Ⓐ the cat

Ⓑ the dog

Ⓒ Sid

3. Why is Sid sad?

Ⓐ It is hot.

Ⓑ There is a cat.

Ⓒ He is tired.

1. ☺ ☹

2. ☺ ☹

3. ☺ ☹

4. ☺ ☹

____ / 4
Total

2. Where is Sid?

Ⓐ on a cat

Ⓑ in a hut

Ⓒ on a mat

4. Which is another good title?

Ⓐ Three in a Hut

Ⓑ Meet on a Mat

Ⓒ Cat and Dog

Name: _____ Date: _____

SCORE

____ / 4
Total

Directions Look at the story. What happens next? Finish the story with a picture. Label the picture.

Peg has two pets.

Peg pats the dog.

#50921—180 Days of Reading for Kindergarten   © Shell Education

Name: _____ **Date:** _____

Directions Match the words to the pictures.

tap   tip   top

 **1.** top

 2. tap

 3. tip

Directions Circle the word for the picture. Write the word.

4.

_____ _____ _____

– – – – –

_____ _____ _____

tag   tan

Name: _____ Date: _____

SCORE

1. 😊 😐

2. 😊 😐

3. 😊 😐

4. 😊 😐

_____ / 4
Total

Directions Match the words to the pictures.

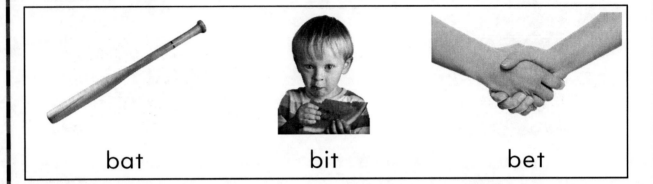

bat   bit   bet

1. bat

2. bet

3. bit

Directions Circle the word for the picture.
Write the word.

4.

_____ _____ _____

- - - - - - - -

_____ _____ _____

Ben   bug

Name: _____ **Date:** _____

Directions Match the words to the pictures.

cat   cut   cot

1. ☺ 😐

2. ☺ 😐

3. ☺ 😐

1. cot

2. cut

3. cat

4. ☺ 😐

____ / 4
Total

Directions Circle the word for the picture.
Write the word.

4.

_____ _____ _____

- - - - - - - - - - - -

_____ _____ _____

can   cap

Name: _____ **Date:** _____

Play Tag

tag

Pam and Sam play tag.

ran

Pam ran fast.

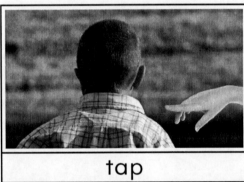

tap

Pam can tap Sam.

Sam

Sam is "It"!

    © Shell Education

Name: _____ Date: _____

Directions Listen to and read "Play Tag." Answer the questions.

1. Who plays tag?

(A) Pam

(B) Sam

(C) Pam and Sam

3. Why is Sam "It"?

(A) Pam ran fast.

(B) Pam taps Sam.

(C) Sam plays tag.

2. Who ran fast?

(A) Sam

(B) Pam

(C) Pam and Sam

4. What is this story about?

(A) playing tag

(B) Sam

(C) running fast

Name: _____ Date: _____

SCORE

____ / 4
Total

Directions Look at the story. What happens next? Finish the story with a picture. Label the picture.

The cat
sees a cot.

The cat
cut the cot.

Bad cat!

Name: _____   **Date:** _____

Directions Match the words to the pictures.

SCORE

1. ☺ ☺

2. ☺ ☺

3. ☺ ☺

4. ☺ ☺

____ / 4
Total

crab   band   lamp

1. band

2. lamp

3. crab

Directions Circle the word for the picture.
Write the word.

4.

___ ___ ___ ___

___ ___ ___ ___

___ ___ ___ ___

flag   hand

Name: _____ **Date:** _____

SCORE

1. ☺ ☹

2. ☺ ☹

3. ☺ ☹

4. ☺ ☹

____ / 4
Total

Directions Match the words to the pictures.

hang   mask   sang

1. sang

2. hang

3. mask

Directions Circle the word for the picture.
Write the word.

4.

_____ _____ _____ _____

_____ _____ _____ _____

bang   bank

Name: _____ Date: _____

Directions Match the words to the pictures.

hand glad clap

1. glad

2. clap

3. hand

Directions Circle the word for the picture.
Write the word.

4.    _____ _____ _____ _____

camp   trap

Name: _____ Date: _____

Camping

Sam and Pam love to camp at the beach.

They swim.

Dad makes a campfire.

They fix hot dogs.

Yum!

 © Shell Education

Name: _____ **Date:** _____

Directions Listen to and read "Camping."
Answer the questions.

---

1. Who makes the campfire?

  Ⓐ Sam

  Ⓑ Pam

  Ⓒ Dad

3. How do the hot dogs taste?

  Ⓐ bad

  Ⓑ okay

  Ⓒ very good

2. Where do they camp?

  Ⓐ at the beach

  Ⓑ at the forest

  Ⓒ at the backyard

4. What is this story about?

  Ⓐ swimming

  Ⓑ camping at the beach

  Ⓒ making hot dogs

Name: _____ Date: _____

SCORE

____ / 4
Total

Directions Look at the story. What happens next? Finish the story with a picture. Label the picture.

Here comes a flag.

Here comes a man in a mask.

Here comes a band.

#50921—180 Days of Reading for Kindergarten   © Shell Education

Name: _____ **Date:** _____

Directions Match the words to the pictures.

ring   clip   mint

1. ☺ 😐

2. ☺ 😐

3. ☺ 😐

1. clip

4. ☺ 😐

____ / 4
Total

2. mint

3. ring

Directions Circle the word for the picture.
Write the word.

4.

___ ___ ___ ___

‑ ‑ ‑ ‑ ‑ ‑ ‑

___ ___ ___ ___

swim   drip

Name: _____ **Date:** _____

SCORE

1.

2.

3.

4.

____ / 4
Total

Directions Match the words to the pictures.

fist   sing   crib

1. crib

2. fist

3. sing

Directions Circle the word for the picture.
Write the word.

4.

____ ____ ____ ____

_ _ _ _ _ _ _ _

____ ____ ____ ____

mist   lift

Name: _____ **Date:** _____

Directions Match the words to the pictures.

grin   sink   twig

1. sink

2. grin

3. twig

Directions Circle the word for the picture.
Write the word.

4.

_____ _____ _____ _____

_ _ _ _ _ _ _ _

_____ _____ _____ _____

milk   wink

Name: _____ **Date:** _____

The Singer's Ring

ring

The ring is nice.

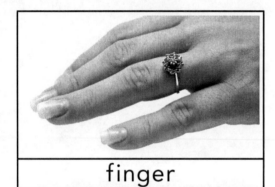

finger

She wears it on her finger.

sing

She wears it to sing.

grin

She grins when she sings.

Name: _____ Date: _____

Directions Listen to and read "The Singer's Ring." Answer the questions.

1. What is nice?

 Ⓐ the ring

 Ⓑ the song

 Ⓒ the lady

3. When does she wear the ring?

 Ⓐ all the time

 Ⓑ when she flips

 Ⓒ when she sings

2. When does she grin?

 Ⓐ when she sits

 Ⓑ when she rings

 Ⓒ when she sings

4. Which is another good title?

 Ⓐ A Nice Lady

 Ⓑ A Nice Ring

 Ⓒ A Nice Song

Name: _____ **Date:** _____

SCORE

___ / 4
Total

Directions Look at the story. What happens next? Finish the story with a picture. Label the picture.

He gets some milk.

She sings to him.

He is in the crib.

Name: _____   Date: _____

Directions Match the words to the pictures.

SCORE

1. 🙂 😐

2. 🙂 😐

3. 🙂 😐

4. 🙂 😐

____ / 4
Total

frog   boss   song

1. boss

2. song

3. frog

Directions Circle the word for the picture.
Write the word.

4.

_____ _____ _____ _____

_ _ _ _ _ _ _ _ _ _

_____ _____ _____ _____

pond   toss

Name: _____ Date: _____

SCORE

1. ☺ ☹

2. ☺ ☹

3. ☺ ☹

4. ☺ ☹

_____ / 4
Total

Directions Match the words to the pictures.

stop   chop   lock

1. stop

2. chop

3. lock

Directions Circle the word for the picture. Write the word.

4.

__ __ __ __

__ __ __ __

__ __ __

dock   crop

Name: _____ **Date:** _____

Directions Match the words to the pictures.

 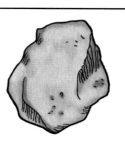

spot   shop   rock

1. spot

2. rock

3. shop

Directions Circle the word for the picture.
Write the word.

4.

___ ___ ___ ___

___ ___ ___

___ ___ ___ ___

lock   drop

Name: _____   **Date:** _____

The Ox

An ox can pull a rock.

It can pull a log.

It can help with a crop.

An ox is strong!

   #50921—180 Days of Reading for Kindergarten   © Shell Education

Name: _____ Date: _____

Directions Listen to and read "The Ox." Answer the questions.

SCORE

1. ☺ 😐

1. What animal is this story about?

Ⓐ an ox

Ⓑ a log

Ⓒ a cat

3. Who does the ox help?

Ⓐ the rock

Ⓑ a farmer

Ⓒ another ox

2. ☺ 😐

3. ☺ 😐

2. What can an ox pull?

Ⓐ a crop

Ⓑ a rock

Ⓒ a baby

4. Which is another good title?

Ⓐ Strong Ox

Ⓑ Move Rocks

Ⓒ Animals

4. ☺ 😐

____ / 4
Total

Name: _____ Date: _____

SCORE

____ / 4
Total

Directions Look at the story. What happens next? Finish the story with a picture. Label the picture.

The frog is by a pond.

He jumps to a rock.

The frog sings a song. Ribbit!

#50921—180 Days of Reading for Kindergarten   © Shell Education

Name: _____ **Date:** _____

Directions Match the words to the pictures.

tent   bell   nest

1. ☺ 😐

2. ☺ 😐

3. ☺ 😐

1.  nest

4. ☺ 😐

____ / 4
Total

2. tent

3. bell

Directions Circle the word for the picture.
Write the word.

4.

     ___ ___ ___ ___

     _ _ _ _ _ _ _

     ___ ___ ___ ___

test   bend

© Shell Education

Name: _____ Date: _____

SCORE

1. 😊 😐

2. 😊 😐

3. 😊 😐

4. 😊 😐

_____ / 4
Total

Directions Match the words to the pictures.

  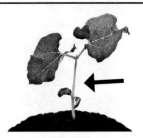

cent   left   stem

1. left

2. stem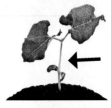

3. cent

Directions Circle the word for the picture. Write the word.

4.

___ ___ ___ ___

_ _ _ _ _ _ _

___ ___ ___ ___

vest   dent

#50921—180 Days of Reading for Kindergarten   © Shell Education

Name: _____ **Date:** _____

Directions Match the words to the pictures.

send   belt   help

1. belt

2. help

3. send

Directions Circle the word for the picture.
Write the word.

4.

_____ _____ _____ _____

— — — — — — — — — —

_____ _____ _____ _____

west   well

Name: _____ Date: _____

Ed and Meg Go Camping

camp

Ed and Meg get ready to camp.

tent

Ed gets a tent.

bed

Meg gets a bed.

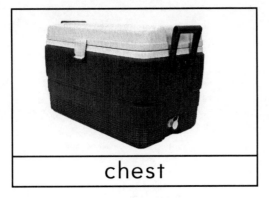

chest

They get food in the chest.

#50921—180 Days of Reading for Kindergarten

© Shell Education

Name: _____   **Date:** _____

Directions Listen to and read "Ed and Meg Go Camping." Answer the questions.

1. Who is going camping?

Ⓐ the tent

Ⓑ Ed

Ⓒ Ed and Meg

3. Why do Ed and Meg need a tent?

Ⓐ They will spend the night.

Ⓑ They will eat.

Ⓒ They will come home.

2. Who gets a bed?

Ⓐ Ed

Ⓑ Meg

Ⓒ Mom

4. What is this story about?

Ⓐ getting ready to eat

Ⓑ getting ready to camp

Ⓒ getting ready for school

SCORE

1. ☺ ☺

2. ☺ ☺

3. ☺ ☺

4. ☺ ☺

___ / 4
Total

Name: _____   Date: _____

SCORE

____ / 4
Total

Directions Look at the story. What happens next? Finish the story with a picture. Label the picture.

Kent put on his vest.

He goes out of the tent.

Kent sees a nest.

Name: _____ **Date:** _____

Directions Match the words to the pictures.

SCORE

1. ☺ 😐

2. ☺ 😐

3. ☺ 😐

4. ☺ 😐

____ / 4
Total

drum   plug   junk boat

1. plug

2. drum

3. junk boat

Directions Circle the word for the picture.
Write the word.

4.  _____ _____ _____ _____

‑ ‑ ‑ ‑ ‑ ‑ ‑ ‑ ‑ ‑ ‑ ‑ ‑ ‑

_____ _____ _____

bunk   slug

Name: _____ Date: _____

SCORE

1. ☺ ☹

2. ☺ ☹

3. ☺ ☹

4. ☺ ☹

____ / 4
Total

Directions Match the words to the pictures.

slug   plus   hung

1. plus

2. hung

3. slug

Directions Circle the word for the picture.
Write the word.

4.

hunt   duck

____ ____ ____ ____

- - - - - - - -

____ ____ ____ ____

#50921—180 Days of Reading for Kindergarten   © Shell Education

Name: _____ **Date:** _____

Directions Match the words to the pictures.

plum   dust   jump

1. dust

2. jump

3. plum

Directions Circle the word for the picture.
Write the word.

4.

_____ _____ _____ _____

_ _ _ _ _ _ _ _

_____ _____ _____ _____

dunk   rung

Name: _____ Date: _____

The Sea

junk boat

tug

sub

A sub goes under the sea.

A junk boat goes on the sea.

A tug pulls big boats.

Chug, chug, chug!

Name: _____   **Date:** _____

SCORE

Directions Listen to and read "The Sea."
Answer the questions.

1. Which boat goes under the sea?

(A) sub

(B) junk

(C) tug

3. What is a junk?

(A) a kind of boat

(B) a kind of sub

(C) a kind of car

2. How does a tug help?

(A) it goes under the sea

(B) it holds people

(C) it pulls big boats

4. What is this story about?

(A) kinds of water

(B) kinds of boats

(C) kinds of workers

1. ☺ ☹

2. ☺ ☹

3. ☺ ☹

4. ☺ ☹

____ / 4
Total

Name: _____   Date: _____

SCORE

___ / 4
Total

Directions Look at the story. What happens next? Finish the story with a picture. Label the picture.

Gus has a bunk bed.

He goes on the top.

Gus jumps on the bed.

Name: _____ **Date:** _____

SCORE

Directions Match the words to the pictures.

car   cart   yard

1. 😊 😐

2. 😊 😐

3. 😊 😐

4. 😊 😐

____ / 4
Total

 cart

 yard

 car

Directions Circle the word for the picture.
Write the word.

4.

bark   farm

_____ _____ _____ _____

—— —— —— ——

_____ _____ _____ _____

Name: _____ **Date:** _____

SCORE

1. ☺ ☹

2. ☺ ☹

3. ☺ ☹

4. ☺ ☹

____ / 4
Total

Directions Match the words to the pictures.

jar   star   dart

1. star

2. jar

3. dart

Directions Circle the word for the picture.
Write the word.

4.

___ ___ ___ ___

_ _ _ _ _

___ ___ ___ ___

arm   harp

Name: _____ **Date:** _____

Directions Match the words to the pictures.

barn   card   farm

1. card

2. farm

3. barn

Directions Circle the word for the picture.
Write the word.

4.    ___ ___ ___ ___

yard   tarp

SCORE

1. ☺ ☺
2. ☺ ☺
3. ☺ ☺
4. ☺ ☺

___/ 4
Total

Name: _____ **Date:** _____

Cats Have Fun

car

Two cats get in a car.

cart

One cat gets in a cart.

yarn

One cat gets in the yarn.

jar

No cat! Not in the jam jar!

© Shell Education

Name: _____ Date: _____

Directions Listen to and read "Cats Have Fun."
Answer the questions.

1. What are the cats doing?

Ⓐ driving

Ⓑ playing

Ⓒ sewing

3. Why should the cat **not** get in the jar?

Ⓐ It is sticky.

Ⓑ It is fun.

Ⓒ It is big.

2. Where does one cat go?

Ⓐ in a cart

Ⓑ in the house

Ⓒ in the bed

4. Which is another good title?

Ⓐ Cats

Ⓑ Animals

Ⓒ Going Places

Name: _____ Date: _____

SCORE

___ / 4
Total

Directions Look at the story. What happens next? Finish the story with a picture. Label the picture.

We got in
the car.

We went
to a farm.

We went
in the barn.

Name: _____ **Date:** _____

Directions Match the words to the pictures.

bin   bird   dirt

1. bin

2. dirt

3. bird

Directions Circle the word for the picture.
Write the word.

4.

_____ _____ _____

– – – – – – – – – – – –

_____ _____ _____

sir   tin

Name: _____ Date: _____

SCORE

1. 🙂 😐

2. 🙂 😐

3. 🙂 😐

4. 🙂 😐

_____ / 4
Total

Directions Match the words to the pictures.

stick   stir   girl

 1. stir

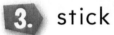 **2.** girl

3. stick

Directions Circle the word for the picture.
Write the word.

4.  _____

_____

_____

third   dirty

#50921—180 Days of Reading for Kindergarten   © Shell Education

Name: _____ **Date:** _____

SCORE

Directions Match the words to the pictures.

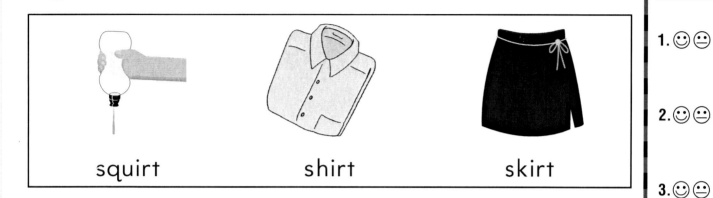

squirt   shirt   skirt

1. ☺ ☺

2. ☺ ☺

3. ☺ ☺

4. ☺ ☺

____ / 4
Total

1. skirt

2. shirt

3. squirt

Directions Circle the word for the picture.
Write the word.

4.

_____ _____ _____ _____

_ _ _ _ _ _ _ _ _ _ _ _

_____ _____ _____ _____

girls   first

Name: _____   Date: _____

Fun in the Dirt

The girl digs in the dirt.

The girl gets a hose. Squirt! Squirt!

The girl stirs the dirt with a stick.

The girl can fill her pan with mud!

#50921—180 Days of Reading for Kindergarten   © Shell Education

Name: _____ Date: _____

> **Directions** Listen to and read "Fun in the Dirt."
> Answer the questions.

1. Who is playing in the dirt?

   (A) a stick

   (B) the girl

   (C) some children

3. Where is the girl?

   (A) in the house

   (B) in her room

   (C) outside

2. Why does the story say *Squirt*?

   (A) that is the water coming out of the hose

   (B) the girl gets sprayed

   (C) the girl is drinking

4. Which is another good title?

   (A) Eating Mud

   (B) Digging in the Dirt

   (C) Pans

1. ☺ ☺

2. ☺ ☺

3. ☺ ☺

4. ☺ ☺

_____ / 4
Total

Name: _____ Date: _____

SCORE

_____ / 4
Total

Directions Look at the story. What happens next? Finish the story with a picture. Label the picture.

First the bird gets up.   Then he digs in the dirt.

Name: _____   **Date:** _____

Directions Match the words to the pictures.

horn   torn   worn

SCORE

1. ☺ ☺

2. ☺ ☺

3. ☺ ☺

4. ☺ ☺

____ / 4
Total

1. torn

2. worn

3. horn

Directions Circle the word for the picture.
Write the word.

4.

___ ___ ___ ___

─ ─ ─ ─ ─ ─

___ ___ ___ ___

corn   fort

Name: _____ Date: _____

SCORE

1. ☺ ☹

2. ☺ ☹

3. ☺ ☹

4. ☺ ☹

____ / 4
Total

Directions Match the words to the pictures.

cork   port   stork

1. cork

2. stork

3. port

Directions Circle the word for the picture.
Write the word.

4.

____ ____ ____ ____

_ _ _ _ _ _ _ _ _ _

____ ____ ____ ____

fork   torn

Name: _____   Date: _____

Directions Match the words to the pictures.

fort   porch   torch

1. ☺ 😐

2. ☺ 😐

3. ☺ 😐

1. torch

4. ☺ 😐

2. porch

____ / 4
Total

3. fort

Directions Circle the word for the picture.
Write the word.

4.

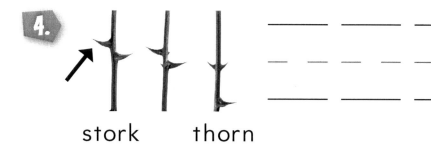

_____ _____ _____ _____ _____

_____ _____ _____ _____ _____

_____ _____ _____ _____ _____

stork   thorn

Name: _____ Date: _____

Dora Makes a Fort

porch

Dora is on the front porch.

fort

Dora makes a fort.

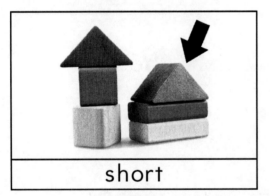

short

The fort is short.

This will work!

#50921—180 Days of Reading for Kindergarten © Shell Education

Name: _____ Date: _____

Directions Listen to and read "Dora Makes a Fort." Answer the questions.

SCORE

1. ☺ ☺

2. ☺ ☺

3. ☺ ☺

4. ☺ ☺

___ / 4
Total

1. Who is the character?

Ⓐ the fort

Ⓑ the porch

Ⓒ Dora

3. What will Dora do with more blocks?

Ⓐ build the fort taller

Ⓑ make the fort fall

Ⓒ make a road

2. What does Dora do?

Ⓐ builds a fort

Ⓑ builds a porch

Ⓒ works

4. What is this story about?

Ⓐ a girl playing in a fort

Ⓑ a girl playing with blocks

Ⓒ a girl and her brother

Name: _____ Date: _____

SCORE

____ / 4
Total

Directions Look at the story. What happens next? Finish the story with a picture. Label the picture.

Norm gets corn.

Then he gets a fork.

_____

— — — — — — — — — — — — — — —

_____

Name: _____   **Date:** _____

SCORE

Directions Match the words to the pictures.

fern   fur   burn

1. ☺ ☺
2. ☺ ☺
3. ☺ ☺
4. ☺ ☺

1. burn

____ / 4
Total

2. fur

3. fern

Directions Circle the word for the picture.
Write the word.

4.    ___ ___ ___ ___

turn   curl

Name: _____ Date: _____

SCORE

1. ☺ ☹

2. ☺ ☹

3. ☺ ☹

4. ☺ ☹

____ / 4
Total

Directions Match the words to the pictures.

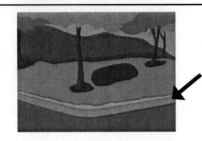  

curb   curl   spur

1. curl

2. spur

3. curb

Directions Circle the word for the picture.
Write the word.

4.

_____ _____ _____ _____

_ _ _ _ _ _ _ _ _

_____ _____ _____ _____

surf   burn

Name: _____ **Date:** _____

Directions Match the words to the pictures.

SCORE

nurse   purse   church

1. ☺ ☻

2. ☺ ☻

3. ☺ ☻

4. ☺ ☻

1. nurse

____ / 4
Total

2. church

3. purse

Directions Circle the word for the picture.
Write the word.

4.

— — — — — —

- - - - - - -

— — — — — —

purple   turtle

Name: _____   **Date:** _____

Fern Falls

Fern fell on the curb.

Ow! That hurt!

Mom can fix that.

Mom is a good nurse!

    #50921—180 Days of Reading for Kindergarten   © Shell Education

Name: _____   **Date:** _____

Directions   Listen to and read "Fern Falls."
Answer the questions.

1. Who fell?

Ⓐ Fern

Ⓑ Mom

Ⓒ the curb

2. What happened
when Fern fell?

Ⓐ She fixed the curb.

Ⓑ She hurt herself.

Ⓒ She went to
a nurse.

3. How did Mom help?

Ⓐ She gave Fern
a bandage.

Ⓑ She picked Fern up.

Ⓒ She fell, too.

4. What is this
story about?

Ⓐ a girl falling and
her mom helping

Ⓑ a girl who got hurt

Ⓒ a mom who is
a nurse

1. ☺ ☹

2. ☺ ☹

3. ☺ ☹

4. ☺ ☹

____ / 4
Total

Name: _____ Date: _____

SCORE

____ / 4
Total

Directions Look at the story. What happens next? Finish the story with a picture. Label the picture.

The wave can turn.

The wave can curl.

Dad wants to surf.

#50921—180 Days of Reading for Kindergarten   © Shell Education

Name: _____ **Date:** _____

SCORE

Directions Match the words to the pictures.

 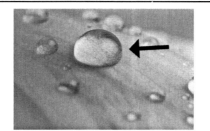 

dress   drop   drum

1. ☺ ☺

2. ☺ ☺

3. ☺ ☺

4. ☺ ☺

____ / 4
Total

1. drop

2. dress

3. drum

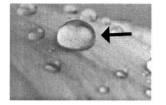

Directions Circle the word for the picture.
Write the word.

4.

_____ _____ _____ _____

‑ ‑ ‑ ‑ ‑ ‑ ‑ ‑ ‑

_____ _____ _____ _____

drag   drip

Name: _____ Date: _____

SCORE

1. ☺ ☹

2. ☺ ☹

3. ☺ ☹

4. ☺ ☹

____ / 4
Total

Directions Match the words to the pictures.

drill   drink   drip

1. drip

2. drink

3. drill

Directions Circle the word for the picture. Write the word.

4.

___ ___ ___ ___

_ _ _ _ _ _ _ _

___ ___ ___ ___

draw   drop

#50921—180 Days of Reading for Kindergarten
© Shell Education

Name: _____ Date: _____

Directions Match the words to the pictures.

frog   grin   grass

1. grin

2. grass

3. frog

Directions Circle the word for the picture.
Write the word.

4.    ___ ___ ___ ___

          — — — — —

          ___ ___ ___ ___

from   grab

Name: _____   Date: _____

Fran's New Dress

dress

Fran has a new dress.

drink

She sips a drink.

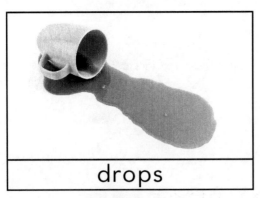

drops

Fran drops the drink.

Oh, no! It's on her dress!

© Shell Education

Name: _____ **Date:** _____

Directions Listen to and read "Fran's New Dress." Answer the questions.

---

1. Who has a new dress?

Ⓐ a drink

Ⓑ Fran

Ⓒ Fred

---

3. What happens when Fran drops the drink?

Ⓐ she sips the drink

Ⓑ she gets a new drink

Ⓒ it gets on her dress

---

2. What does Fran do?

Ⓐ sips a drink

Ⓑ shows her dress

Ⓒ falls down

---

4. Which is another good title?

Ⓐ The Big Splat

Ⓑ Juice

Ⓒ Drinks

---

1. ☺ 😐

2. ☺ 😐

3. ☺ 😐

4. ☺ 😐

____ / 4
Total

Name: _____ **Date:** _____

SCORE

____ / 4
Total

Directions Look at the story. What happens next? Finish the story with a picture. Label the picture.

Fred can draw a crab.   He can draw a frog.

_____

- -

_____

#50921—180 Days of Reading for Kindergarten   © Shell Education

Name: _____ **Date:** _____

Directions Match the words to the pictures.

SCORE

 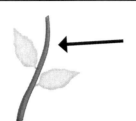 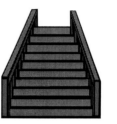

stop   stem   step

1. ☺ ☹

2. ☺ ☹

3. ☺ ☹

4. ☺ ☹

_____ / 4
Total

1. step

2. stem

3. stop

Directions Circle the word for the picture.
Write the word.

4.

— — — — — — — —

– – – – – – – –

— — — — — — — —

stick   start

Name: _____ Date: _____

SCORE

1. ☺ ☹

2. ☺ ☹

3. ☺ ☹

4. ☺ ☹

____ / 4
Total

Directions Match the words to the pictures.

star   stamp   stump

1. stump

2. star

3. stamp

Directions Circle the word for the picture.
Write the word.

4.

___ ___ ___ ___ ___

- - - - - -

___ ___ ___ ___ ___

sting   stand

Name: _____ **Date:** _____

Directions Match the words to the pictures.

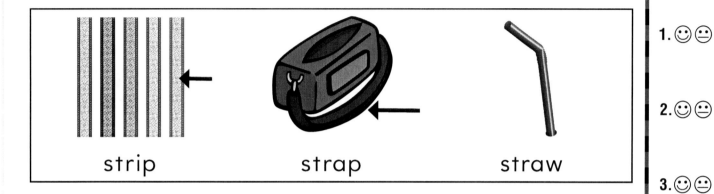

strip   strap   straw

1. strap

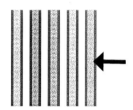

2. straw

3. strip

Directions Circle the word for the picture.
Write the word.

4.

——— ——— ——— ——— ——— ———

– – – – – – – – – – – – – – – – – – – –

——— ——— ——— ——— ——— ———

stripe   string

Name: _____ Date: _____

Stan and the Stump

Stan steps down the path.

Stan stops at a stump.

Stan steps up on the stump.

Stan still cannot get a star.

#50921—180 Days of Reading for Kindergarten   © Shell Education

Name: _____ Date: _____

Directions Listen to and read "Stan and the Stump." Answer the questions.

1. Who goes for a walk?

(A) the stump

(B) Sid

(C) Stan

3. What time of day is it?

(A) daytime

(B) nighttime

(C) morning

2. What is a stump?

(A) a cut-off tree

(B) a star

(C) a path

4. Which is another good title?

(A) Nighttime

(B) Steps

(C) Reaching High

1. ☺ ☺

2. ☺ ☺

3. ☺ ☺

4. ☺ ☺

____ / 4
Total

Name: _____ Date: _____

SCORE

___ / 4
Total

Directions Look at the story. What happens next? Finish the story with a picture. Label the picture.

Dad sees some sticks.

He straps the sticks.

Dad sees some straw.

Name: _____ Date: _____

Directions Match the words to the pictures.

sack

snack

snap

1. ☺ ☻

2. ☺ ☻

3. ☺ ☻

1. snack

4. ☺ ☻

2. snap

____ / 4
Total

3. sack

Directions Circle the word for the picture.
Write the word.

4.

——— ——— ——— ———

– – – – – – – –

——— ——— ——— ———

snip   snarl

Name: _____ **Date:** _____

SCORE

1.

2.

3.

4.

_____ / 4
Total

Directions Match the words to the pictures.

sled   slip   slug

 1. slip

 2. slug

3. sled

Directions Circle the word for the picture.
Write the word.

4.

slick   slice

___ ___ ___ ___ ___ ___

_ _ _ _ _ _ _

___ ___ ___ ___ ___ ___

Name: _____ **Date:** _____

Directions Match the words to the pictures.

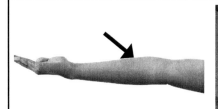  

skin   skip   skunk

1. skunk

2. skip

3. skin

Directions Circle the word for the picture.
Write the word.

4.

——— ——— ——— ———

– – – – – – – – – – –

——— ——— ——— ———

skit   spot

Name: _____ **Date:** _____

Skipping Sal

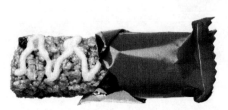

snack

Sal has a snack in her sack.

skips

She skips on the path.

Sal looks for a spot to stop.

skunk

Don't stop by that skunk!

© Shell Education

Name: _____ **Date:** _____

Directions Listen to and read "Skipping Sal." Answer the questions.

1. Who goes for a walk?

(A) Sal

(B) skunk

(C) skip

3. Why should she **not** stop by the skunk?

(A) It will eat her snack.

(B) It will get in her sack.

(C) It may spray her.

2. What is Sal doing?

(A) She is taking a walk.

(B) She is looking for skunks.

(C) She is stopping.

4. Which is another good title?

(A) Skunk on the Path

(B) The Giant Snack

(C) The ABCs

Name: _____ Date: _____

SCORE

_____ / 4
Total

Directions Look at the story. What happens next? Finish the story with a picture. Label the picture.

Sam sees the snow.

He grabs his sled.

Sam spots a hill.

Name: _____ **Date:** _____

Directions Match the words to the pictures.

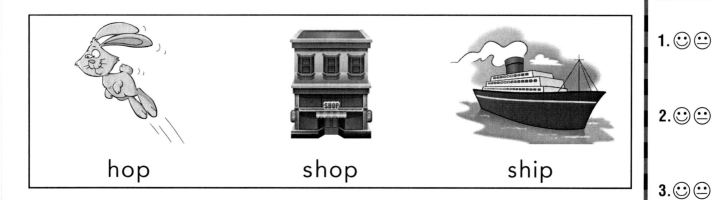

hop   shop   ship

SCORE

1. 🙂 😐

2. 🙂 😐

3. 🙂 😐

4. 🙂 😐

____ / 4
Total

1. hop

2. ship

3. shop

Directions Circle the word for the picture.
Write the word.

4.

_____ _____ _____ _____

_ _ _ _ _ _ _ _ _

_____ _____ _____ _____

shut   sell

Name: _____ **Date:** _____

SCORE

1. 😊 😐

2. 😊 😐

3. 😊 😐

4. 😊 😐

____ / 4
Total

Directions Match the words to the pictures.

sack   shack   shark

1. shark

2. shack

3. sack

Directions Circle the word for the picture.
Write the word.

4.

___ ___ ___ ___ ___ ___ ___

___ ___ ___ ___ ___ ___ ___

___ ___ ___ ___ ___ ___ ___

sheep   stick

Name: _____ **Date:** _____

Directions Match the words to the pictures.

 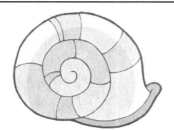 

shed   shell   shelf

1. shelf

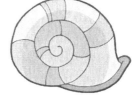

2. shed

3. shell

Directions Circle the word for the picture.
Write the word.

4.

___ ___ ___ ___ ___

___ ___ ___ ___ ___

sharp   shirt

Name: _____ Date: _____

Shad Shops

Shad shops on his trip.

He sees shells on a shelf.

Shad sees a ship and shark teeth.

Shad wants it all!

 #50921—180 Days of Reading for Kindergarten © Shell Education

Name: _____ Date: _____

Directions Listen to and read "Shad Shops." Answer the questions.

1. Who is shopping?

Ⓐ the shelf

Ⓑ Shad

Ⓒ shark teeth

3. Why does Shad want it all?

Ⓐ He wants shark teeth.

Ⓑ He likes everything he sees.

Ⓒ He is on a trip.

2. Where does Shad see the shells?

Ⓐ in a bottle

Ⓑ on a shelf

Ⓒ in the shark teeth

4. What is this story about?

Ⓐ a boy who is shopping

Ⓑ a boy who is on a ship

Ⓒ a boy looking for shells

1. ☺ ☺

2. ☺ ☺

3. ☺ ☺

4. ☺ ☺

____ / 4
Total

Name: _____ **Date:** _____

SCORE

____ / 4
Total

Directions Look at the story. What happens next? Finish the story with a picture. Label the picture.

The sheep is in the pen.

Oh no!
The pen is not shut!

#50921—180 Days of Reading for Kindergarten   © Shell Education

Name: _____ **Date:** _____

Directions Match the words to the pictures.

SCORE

chin   chip   chimp

1.☺☻

2.☺☻

3.☺☻

1. chimp

4.☺☻

2. chip

____ / 4
Total

3. chin

Directions Circle the word for the picture.
Write the word.

4.

___ ___ ___ ___ ___

___ ___ ___ ___ ___

___ ___ ___ ___ ___

cheek   chat

Name: _____ **Date:** _____

SCORE

1. 😊 😐

2. 😊 😐

3. 😊 😐

4. 😊 😐

___ / 4
Total

Directions Match the words to the pictures.

chick   check   chest

1. chest

2. check

3. chick

Directions Circle the word for the picture. Write the word.

4.

— — — — — — —

— — — — — — —

— — — — — — —

child   cherry

Name: _____ **Date:** _____

SCORE

Directions Match the words to the pictures.

chop

chart

chirp

1. ☺ ☺

2. ☺ ☺

3. ☺ ☺

4. ☺ ☺

____ / 4
Total

1. chirp

2. chart

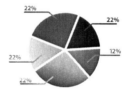

3. chop

Directions Circle the word for the picture.
Write the word.

4.

chess   chant

___ ___ ___ ___ ___

_ _ _ _ _ _

___ ___ ___ ___ ___

Name: _____ **Date:** _____

The Chimp

Char

Char checks on the chimp.

chest

The chimp thumps its chest.

chin

The chimp scratches its chin.

chimp

The chimp likes its chum.

 #50921—180 Days of Reading for Kindergarten © Shell Education

Name: _____ **Date:** _____

Directions Listen to and read "The Chimp."
Answer the questions.

---

1. Who checks on the chimp?

Ⓐ chum

Ⓑ Char

Ⓒ Cheryl

3. What is Char's job?

Ⓐ to be a chum

Ⓑ to work with chimps

Ⓒ to be a zoo visitor

2. What does the chimp do?

Ⓐ thumps its chest

Ⓑ swings from trees

Ⓒ checks on Char

4. What is this text about?

Ⓐ a chimp

Ⓑ Char

Ⓒ a chum

Name: _____ Date: _____

SCORE

____ / 4
Total

Directions Look at the story. What happens next? Finish the story with a picture. Label the picture.

The cook checks the chart.

He chops the cherry.

       © Shell Education

Name: _____ **Date:** _____

Directions Match the words to the pictures.

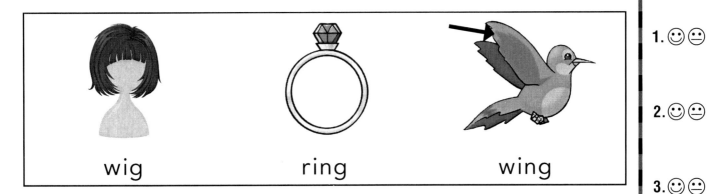

wig   ring   wing

 ring

 wig

3. wing

Directions Circle the word for the picture.
Write the word.

4.

sing   sat

_____ _____ _____ _____

- - - - - - - - - - - -

_____ _____ _____ _____

Name: _____   **Date:** _____

SCORE

1. ☺ ☹

2. ☺ ☹

3. ☺ ☹

4. ☺ ☹

___ / 4
Total

Directions Match the words to the pictures.

 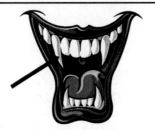 

fan   fang   king

1. fang

2. fan

3. king

Directions Circle the word for the picture.
Write the word.

4.    ___ ___ ___ ___

___ ___ ___ ___

___ ___ ___ ___

hung   hash

Name: _____ **Date:** _____

Directions Match the words to the pictures.

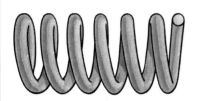      

spring   string   swing

1. swing

2. string

3. spring

Directions Circle the word for the picture.
Write the word.

4.    ___ ___ ___ ___ ___ ___

stands   street

Name: _____ Date: _____

Bing Likes to Swing

Bing gets on the swing.

Bing sings as he swings.

His legs are like springs!

His arms are like wings!

Name: _____ **Date:** _____

Directions Listen to and read "Bing Likes to Swing." Answer the questions.

1. Who gets on the swing?

(A) a bird

(B) a girl

(C) Bing

3. Why does Bing sing?

(A) He is a bird.

(B) He is happy.

(C) He has arms.

2. Where is Bing?

(A) a park

(B) a bedroom

(C) a classroom

4. Which is another good title?

(A) Swinging High

(B) Birds

(C) Funny Legs

Name: _____ Date: _____

SCORE

_____ / 4
Total

Directions Look at the story. What happens next? Finish the story with a picture. Label the picture.

The king has a wig.

He has a ring.

The king gets a fan.

Name: _____   **Date:** _____

Directions Match the words to the pictures.

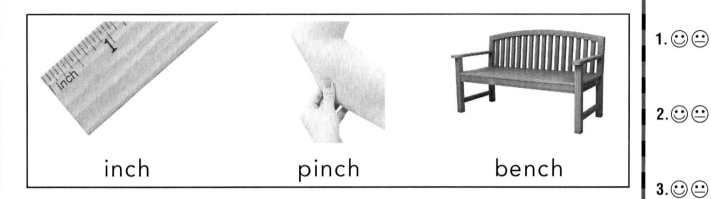

inch   pinch   bench

1. bench

2. pinch

3. inch

Directions Circle the word for the picture.
Write the word.

4.

——— ——— ——— ——— ———

– – – – – – – – – – – – – – –

——— ——— ——— ——— ———

rash   reach

Name: _____ Date: _____

SCORE

1.

2.

3.

4.

_____ / 4
Total

Directions Match the words to the pictures.

   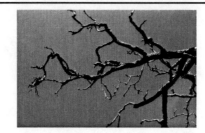   

ranch   branch   lunch

1. branch

2. lunch

3. ranch

Directions Circle the word for the picture.
Write the word.

4.

___ ___ ___ ___

- - - - - - - -

___ ___ ___ ___

rich   ring

 #50921—180 Days of Reading for Kindergarten   © Shell Education

Name: _____ **Date:** _____

SCORE

Directions Match the words to the pictures.

catch   match   pitch

1. ☺ 😐

2. ☺ 😐

1. pitch

3. ☺ 😐

4. ☺ 😐

2. match

____ / 4
Total

3. catch

Directions Circle the word for the picture.
Write the word.

 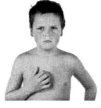

_____ _____ _____ _____

_____ _____ _____ _____ —

_____ _____ _____ _____

inks   itch

Name: _____ Date: _____

Butch on the Ranch

ranch

Butch works on a ranch.

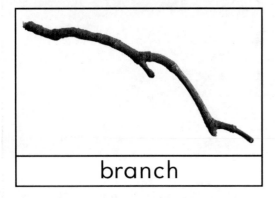

branch

Butch cuts up a big branch.

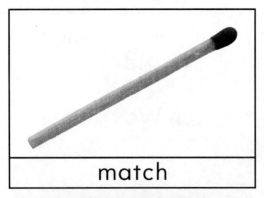

match

Butch gets a bunch of twigs and a match.

lunch

Butch will fix a hot lunch.

 #50921—180 Days of Reading for Kindergarten © Shell Education

Name: _____ Date: _____

Directions Listen to and read "Butch on the Ranch." Answer the questions.

1. Where does Butch work?

(A) on a branch

(B) on a ranch

(C) in a bunch

3. Why does Butch get the twigs and match?

(A) to throw them away

(B) to make a fire

(C) to cut the branch

2. Why does Butch cut the branch?

(A) to get small twigs

(B) to make hot dogs

(C) to help the ranch

4. Which is another good title?

(A) Ranch Work

(B) Hot Dogs

(C) Fire

Name: _____ Date: _____

SCORE

____ / 4
Total

Directions Look at the story. What happens next? Finish the story with a picture. Label the picture.

Can Matt catch the ball?

Sam gets set to pitch.

Matt can reach for the ball.

_____

_ _ _ _ _ _ _ _ _ _ _ _ _ _ _ _ _ _ _

_____

ANSWER KEY

Week 1

Day 1

1. sat
2. bat
3. cat

4. rat

Day 2

1. pat
2. hat
3. fat

4. mat

Day 3

1. van
2. can
3. man

4. fan

Day 4

1.	C	3.	A
2.	B	4.	B

Day 5
Responses will vary.

Week 2

Day 1

1. Pam
2. ham
3. yam

4. jam

Day 2

1. Dad
2. pad
3. bad

4. sad

Day 3

1. map
2. lap
3. nap

4. cap

Day 4

1.	A	3.	B
2.	B	4.	A

Day 5
Responses will vary.

Week 3

Day 1

1. cab
2. can
3. cap

4. cat

Day 2

1. man
2. mad
3. mat

4. map

Day 3

1. tap
2. tan
3. Tad

4. tag

Day 4

1.	C	3.	A
2.	B	4.	A

Day 5
Responses will vary.

ANSWER KEY (cont.)

Week 4

Day 1

1. bag
2. jam
3. Dad

4. wag

Day 2

1. pan
2. lab
3. cab

4. van

Day 3

1. bat
2. ham
3. nap

4. rat

Day 4
1. C   3. B
2. B   4. A

Day 5
Responses will vary.

Week 5

Day 1

1. wig
2. big
3. pig

4. dig

Day 2

1. sit
2. bit
3. hit

4. bit

Day 3

1. bin
2. win
3. pin

4. fin

Day 4
1. A   3. A
2. B   4. C

Day 5
Responses will vary.

Week 6

Day 1

1. bill
2. pill
3. Jill

4. hill

Day 2

1. hip
2. rip
3. lip

4. zip

Day 3

1. sick
2. kick
3. pick

4. lick

Day 4
1. B   3. C
2. A   4. A

Day 5
Responses will vary.

ANSWER KEY *(cont.)*

Week 7

Day 1

1. hid
2. him
3. hit

4. hip

Day 2

1. pick
2. pit
3. pill

4. pin

Day 3

1. bit
2. bib
3. big

4. bin

Day 4

1. A
2. B

3. A
4. B

Day 5
Responses will vary.

Week 8

Day 1

1. hit
2. lip
3. Kim

4. lid

Day 2

1. rip
2. dig
3. six

4. pill

Day 3

1. kid
2. bib
3. fig

4. sick

Day 4

1. B
2. A

3. A
4. C

Day 5
Responses will vary.

Week 9

Day 1

1. top
2. mop
3. pop

4. hop

Day 2

1. hot
2. cot
3. dot

4. pot

Day 3

1. jog
2. hog
3. dog

4. log

Day 4

1. C
2. A

3. B
4. A

Day 5
Responses will vary.

ANSWER KEY *(cont.)*

Week 10

Day 1

1. Don
2. dot
3. dock

4. dog

Day 2

1. cost
2. cop
3. cob

4. cot

Day 3

1. honk
2. hot
3. hog

4. hop

Day 4

1.	A	3.	B
2.	B	4.	A

Day 5
Responses will vary.

Week 11

Day 1

1. box
2. mop
3. rod

4. hog

Day 2

1. dog
2. lock
3. dot

4. fox

Day 3

1. pop
2. jog
3. Mom

4. log

Day 4

1.	B	3.	A
2.	A	4.	A

Day 5
Responses will vary.

Week 12

Day 1

1. men
2. pen
3. hen

4. ten

Day 2

1. net
2. pet
3. jet

4. wet

Day 3

1. Ned
2. red
3. fed

4. bed

Day 4

1.	B	3.	B
2.	A	4.	C

Day 5
Responses will vary.

ANSWER KEY *(cont.)*

Week 13

Day 1

1. beg
2. peg
3. Meg

4. leg

Day 2

1. yell
2. bell
3. fell

4. well

Day 3

1. west
2. nest
3. best

4. vest

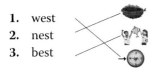

Day 4
1. A   3. B
2. B   4. C

Day 5
Responses will vary.

Week 14

Day 1

1. pest
2. peg
3. pet

4. pen

Day 2

1. bell
2. Ben
3. bed

4. beg

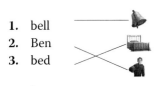

Day 3

1. wet
2. wed
3. well

4. web

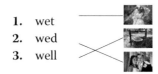

Day 4
1. A   3. B
2. B   4. C

Day 5
Responses will vary.

Week 15

Day 1

1. leg
2. red
3. Ted

4. hen

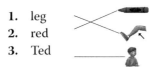

Day 2

1. wet
2. Meg
3. pen

4. jet

Day 3

1. ten
2. vet
3. Ken

4. bed

Day 4
1. C   3. B
2. C   4. B

Day 5
Responses will vary.

ANSWER KEY *(cont.)*

Week 16

Day 1

1. dug
2. rug
3. jug

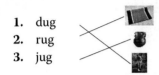

4. bug

Day 2

1. sub
2. rub
3. cub

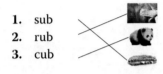

4. tub

Day 3

1. run
2. bun
3. fun

4. sun

Day 4

1. B   3. C
2. A   4. C

Day 5
Responses will vary.

Week 17

Day 1

1. cup
2. cub
3. cud

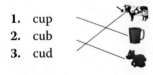

4. cut

Day 2

1. huff
2. hum
3. hug

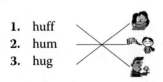

4. hut

Day 3

1. ruff
2. rub
3. run

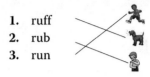

4. rug

Day 4

1. C   3. A
2. A   4. B

Day 5
Responses will vary.

Week 18

Day 1

1. hut
2. mug
3. tug

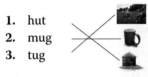

4. cup

Day 2

1. nut
2. pup
3. gum

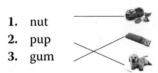

4. hug

Day 3

1. rug
2. Gus
3. cut

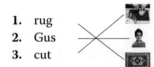

4. bus

Day 4

1. A   3. B
2. C   4. A

Day 5
Responses will vary.

© Shell Education

ANSWER KEY *(cont.)*

Week 19

Day 1

1. hot
2. hit
3. hat

4. hut

Day 2

1. pat
2. pit
3. pot

4. pet

Day 3

1. beg
2. bag
3. big

4. bug

Day 4
1. C   3. A
2. B   4. A

Day 5
Responses will vary.

Week 20

Day 1

1. top
2. tap
3. tip

4. tag

Day 2

1. bat
2. bet
3. bit

4. bug

Day 3

1. cot
2. cut
3. cat

4. can

Day 4
1. C   3. B
2. B   4. A

Day 5
Responses will vary.

Week 21

Day 1

1. band
2. lamp
3. crab

4. flag

Day 2

1. sang
2. hang
3. mask

4. bank

Day 3

1. glad
2. clap
3. hand

4. camp

Day 4
1. C   3. C
2. A   4. B

Day 5
Responses will vary.

ANSWER KEY (cont.)

Week 22

Day 1

1. clip
2. mint
3. ring
4. swim

Day 2

1. crib
2. fist
3. sing
4. lift

Day 3

1. sink
2. grin
3. twig
4. milk

Day 4

1. A
2. C
3. C
4. B

Day 5
Responses will vary.

Week 23

Day 1

1. boss
2. song
3. frog
4. pond

Day 2

1. stop
2. chop
3. lock
4. crop

Day 3

1. spot
2. rock
3. shop
4. drop

Day 4

1. A
2. B
3. B
4. A

Day 5
Responses will vary.

Week 24

Day 1

1. nest
2. tent
3. bell
4. bend

Day 2

1. left
2. stem
3. cent
4. vest

Day 3

1. belt
2. help
3. send
4. west

Day 4

1. C
2. B
3. A
4. B

Day 5
Responses will vary.

ANSWER KEY *(cont.)*

Week 25

Day 1

1. plug
2. drum
3. junk boat

4. bunk

Day 2

1. plus
2. hung
3. slug

4. duck

Day 3

1. dust
2. jump
3. plum

4. dunk

Day 4

1.	A	3.	A
2.	C	4.	B

Day 5
Responses will vary.

Week 26

Day 1

1. cart
2. yard
3. car

4. bark

Day 2

1. star
2. jar
3. dart

4. harp

Day 3

1. card
2. farm
3. barn

4. yard

Day 4

1.	B	3.	A
2.	A	4.	A

Day 5
Responses will vary.

Week 27

Day 1

1. bin
2. dirt
3. bird

4. tin

Day 2

1. stir
2. girl
3. stick

4. third

Day 3

1. skirt
2. shirt
3. squirt

4. first

Day 4

1.	B	3.	C
2.	A	4.	B

Day 5
Responses will vary.

ANSWER KEY *(cont.)*

Week 28

Day 1

1. torn
2. worn
3. horn

4. corn

Day 2

1. cork
2. stork
3. port

4. fork

Day 3

1. torch
2. porch
3. fort

4. thorn

Day 4
1. C   3. A
2. A   4. B

Day 5
Responses will vary.

Week 29

Day 1

1. burn
2. fur
3. fern

4. turn

Day 2

1. curl
2. spur
3. curb

4. surf

Day 3

1. nurse
2. church
3. purse

4. turtle

Day 4
1. A   3. A
2. B   4. A

Day 5
Responses will vary.

Week 30

Day 1

1. drop
2. dress
3. drum

4. drag

Day 2

1. drip
2. drink
3. drill

4. draw

Day 3

1. grin
2. grass
3. frog

4. grab

Day 4
1. B   3. C
2. A   4. A

Day 5
Responses will vary.

ANSWER KEY *(cont.)*

Week 31

Day 1

1. step
2. stem
3. stop
4. stick

Day 2

1. stump
2. star
3. stamp
4. sting

Day 3

1. strap
2. straw
3. strip
4. string

Day 4

1. C
2. A
3. B
4. C

Day 5
Responses will vary.

Week 32

Day 1

1. snack
2. snap
3. sack
4. snip

Day 2

1. slip
2. slug
3. sled
4. slick

Day 3

1. skunk
2. skip
3. skin
4. spot

Day 4

1. A
2. C
3. C
4. A

Day 5
Responses will vary.

Week 33

Day 1

1. hop
2. ship
3. shop
4. shut

Day 2

1. shark
2. shack
3. sack
4. sheep

Day 3

1. shelf
2. shed
3. shell
4. shirt

Day 4

1. B
2. B
3. B
4. A

Day 5
Responses will vary.

ANSWER KEY *(cont.)*

Week 34

Day 1

1. chimp
2. chip
3. chin
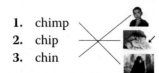

4. cheek

Day 2

1. chest
2. check
3. chick
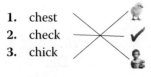

4. cherry

Day 3

1. chirp
2. chart
3. chop
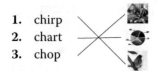

4. chess

Day 4

1.	B	3.	B
2.	A	4.	A

Day 5
Responses will vary.

Week 35

Day 1

1. ring
2. wig
3. wing
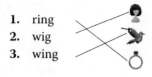

4. sing

Day 2

1. fang
2. fan
3. king
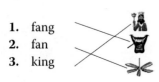

4. hung

Day 3

1. swing
2. string
3. spring

4. street

Day 4

1.	C	3.	B
2.	A	4.	A

Day 5
Responses will vary.

Week 36

Day 1

1. bench
2. pinch
3. inch
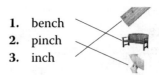

4. reach

Day 2

1. branch
2. lunch
3. ranch
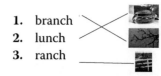

4. rich

Day 3

1. pitch
2. match
3. catch
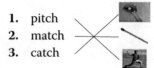

4. itch

Day 4

1.	B	3.	B
2.	A	4.	A

Day 5
Responses will vary.

REFERENCES CITED

Marzano, Robert. 2010. When Practice Makes Perfect…Sense. *Educational Leadership* 68 (3): 81–83.

National Reading Panel. 2000. Report of the National Reading Panel. *Teaching Children to Read: An Evidence-Based Assessment of the Scientific Research Literature on Reading and its Implication for Reading Instruction* (NIH Publication No. 00-4769). Washington, DC: U.S. Government Printing Office.

Rasinski, Timothy V. 2003. *The Fluent Reader: Oral Reading Strategies for Building Word Recognition, Fluency, and Comprehension.* New York: Scholastic.

———. 2006. Fluency: An Oft-Neglected Goal of the Reading Program. In *Understanding and Implementing Reading First Initiatives,* ed. C. Cummins, 60–71. Newark, DE: International Reading Association.

Wolf, Maryanne. 2005. *What is Fluency? Fluency Development: As the Bird Learns to Fly.* Scholastic professional paper. New York: ReadAbout. http://teacher.scholastic.com /products/fluencyformula/pdfs/What_is_Fluency.pdf (accessed June 8, 2007).

CONTENTS OF THE DIGITAL RESOURCE CD

Teacher Resources

Page	Document Title	Filename
4	Standards Correlations Chart	standards.pdf
6	Writing Rubric	writingrubric.pdf writingrubric.doc
7	Fluency Assessment	fluency.pdf
8	Diagnostic Assessment Directions	directions.pdf
10	Practice Page Item Analysis Days 1–3	pageitem1.pdf pageitem1.doc pageitem1.xls
11	Practice Page Item Analysis Days 4–5	pageitem2.pdf pageitem2.doc pageitem2.xls
12	Student Item Analysis Days 1–3	studentitem1.pdf studentitem1.doc studentitem1.xls
13	Student Item Analysis Days 4–5	studentitem2.pdf studentitem2.doc studentitem2.xls

CONTENTS OF THE DIGITAL RESOURCE CD *(cont.)*

Practice Pages

The six practice pages for each week are contained in each PDF. In order to print specific days, open the desired PDF and select the pages to print.

Pages	Week	Filename
15–20	Week 1	week1.pdf
21–26	Week 2	week2.pdf
27–32	Week 3	week3.pdf
33–38	Week 4	week4.pdf
39–44	Week 5	week5.pdf
45–50	Week 6	week6.pdf
51–56	Week 7	week7.pdf
57–62	Week 8	week8.pdf
63–68	Week 9	week9.pdf
69–74	Week 10	week10.pdf
75–80	Week 11	week11.pdf
81–86	Week 12	week12.pdf
87–92	Week 13	week13.pdf
93–98	Week 14	week14.pdf
99–104	Week 15	week15.pdf
105–110	Week 16	week16.pdf
111–116	Week 17	week17.pdf
117–122	Week 18	week18.pdf
123–128	Week 19	week19.pdf
129–134	Week 20	week20.pdf
135–140	Week 21	week21.pdf
141–146	Week 22	week22.pdf
147–152	Week 23	week23.pdf
153–158	Week 24	week24.pdf
159–164	Week 25	week25.pdf
165–170	Week 26	week26.pdf
171–176	Week 27	week27.pdf
177–182	Week 28	week28.pdf
183–188	Week 29	week29.pdf
189–194	Week 30	week30.pdf
195–200	Week 31	week31.pdf
201–206	Week 32	week32.pdf
207–212	Week 33	week33.pdf
213–218	Week 34	week34.pdf
219–224	Week 35	week35.pdf
225–230	Week 36	week36.pdf

NOTES

© Shell Education

NOTES

NOTES

© Shell Education